BREATH OF LIFE

Daniel B. McVey

BREATH OF LIFE

*The Life of a
Volunteer Firefighter*

iUniverse, Inc.
Bloomington

iUniverse books may be ordered through booksellers or by contacting:

iUniverse
1663 Liberty Drive
Bloomington, IN 47403
www.iuniverse.com
1-800-Authors (1-800-288-4677)

ISBN: 978-1-4620-5421-3 (sc)
ISBN: 978-1-4620-5422-0 (hc)
ISBN: 978-1-4620-5423-7 (e)

Library of Congress Control Number: 2011961648

Printed in the United States of America

iUniverse rev. date: 12/13/2011

CONTENTS

PROLOGUE

I WAS BORN AND RAISED in Floral Park, New York. Across the street from where I lived was a firehouse that also housed the Floral Park Active Engine Company. My father was a retired battalion chief in the New York City Fire Department. He was assigned to Downtown Brooklyn on Jay Street. I was around firemen all my life. When I was six, I saw, for the first time, the then new 1964 rescue truck, which was housed a little more than a half a mile from where I lived. It happened sometime in the fall of 1964, when I was playing with some friends on the block. We heard sirens, and I looked up to see the new rescue truck rushing down the road, responding to an emergency. We followed the truck to the emergency scene just a few blocks from where we were playing. I can remember my sister and I approaching to see what was going on.

In my six-year-old mind, I thought it was a fire, so I said to her, "Let's not get too close to the fire." I was afraid of getting hurt.

My sister said, "No, it's an emergency."

Then we heard that a man was having a heart attack. The Nassau County Police ambulance responded and took the patient to the hospital.

Growing up, I was always impressed with the Rescue Company. And by the time I was nine, I had my mind made up that Rescue was my favorite company. The age to enter the volunteer fire department was, at that time, twenty-one. By the time I turned eighteen, the age had been reduced to eighteen, but by then I was no longer interested in joining the fire department. When I was nineteen, I enrolled in a CPR course with my friend Pat, which was taught by some firemen in the Rescue Company, Mike Ostipwko, Garry Gronert, and Terry Carney. We learned that CPR was simply massaging the heart between the sternum (or breastbone) and the spine.

A week after our first class, I was talking to Mrs. Walsh, a crossing guard at the Our Lady of Victory School, where the CPR course was being held. She would help me with my teenage problems, such as those in my "love life" and other things that sometimes parents do not understand. It was May of 1978, and I had just taken my last final exam of the college semester. I was finally on summer vacation. Pat and another friend, Ed, showed up. They stopped to say hello, and all of us talked for a while. Then Mrs. Walsh signed off from her crossing post for the day, and Pat, Ed, and I decided to go to the Village Inn on Tulip Avenue for a few beers. Pat was talking about his love for helping people and said he was looking forward to going to Kentucky with his church group. Pat and I were to have our second CPR class later on that night.

A week later, we had our third and final CPR class, in which I met Father Surlis. He asked me if I attended Saint John's College where he taught theology. I told him that I went to New York Tech in Old Westbury but that he probably recognized me from one of the masses where he served. After class, he and I talked for a little while longer. He was a native of Sligo, Ireland, and spoke with a brogue. We were talking about different things like college and my career goals. Of course, since I was talking to a priest, God was mentioned to some extent. Still, Father Surlis was very humble and talked *to* you as opposed to talking *down* to you. I remember saying something to the extent that I was not good enough for God, and he brought up the fact that I was taking a CPR course in order to help someone in need someday. He made it clear that that was good enough for God.

As the summer of 1978 rolled on, Pat said he might try to get into the Rescue Company. Once, when I stopped by his house, he was working on his garden. I talked to his mother, who was inside the house standing by a large window.

"I think you and Pat should try to join the Emergency Company," she told me. Of course, she meant the Rescue Company. She had taken the CPR course with us.

I had always thought a lot about going into the Rescue Company, but it was all just talk. After I took the CPR course, however, my ambitions to join the company became a little stronger.

Then, several days after my conversation with Pat's mom, Mrs.

Donlon, a friend of Father Surlis called me for a favor. She asked me to drive a man named Peter Walter to a grocery store in New Hyde Park to sell chances for the church. As it turned out, Peter had been a member of the Rescue Company for about two years. He answered some of my questions about the Company and gave me details on how to get into the fire department: I would have to file an application and get three signatures of recommendation from three members of the Rescue Company.

September came and the kids were back to school. I had taken the occasion to stop again to talk to Mrs. Walsh on her crossing post, when Theresa Burns came by to chat with us. I knew Theresa from high school. She was two years younger than I was, and we had always talked about the fire department since her brother was a member of the Hook and Ladder Company. Now, when I mentioned that I was interested in entering the Rescue Company, Theresa was very encouraging, speaking highly of firefighters, whether volunteers or paid. When I left, I went straight to the firehouse on Vernon Street. There, I met First Assistant Chief James Fairben. He told me the requirements for joining the company, such as becoming an Emergency Medical Technician, and told me that Rescue was hurting for manpower in the daytime. I thought I could make a difference in that respect because I was in college and not working, which meant I would be around a lot during the daytime when other members were at their regular jobs. Chief Fairben encouraged me to come down to the firehouse the following Wednesday when Rescue would be having their next drill.

The following Wednesday, I showed up and met a few firefighters from different companies. Eddie Rodriguez from the Alert Engine Company introduced himself and explained certain rules from the bylaws—namely, you had to make 75 percent of all calls during the timeframe that you were available. If you were a day person, you had to make 75 percent of the calls during the day, and if you were a night person, you had to make 75 percent of all calls that occurred during the night. (Not too long after I was sworn in, that rule changed to requiring all members to make 25 percent of all calls that occurred around the clock.) Eddie then introduced me to Ralph Gode, who was a warden for the Rescue Company. (Wardens represented their respective companies at the Fire Council which consisted of the five chiefs and the Fire Commissioner.) Ralph immediately told me that I could sign up for an Emergency Medical Technician (EMT)course at C. W. Post College in Greenvale, in northern Long Island.

Finally, another man came up to me and said, "Are you joining us, Danny?"

"Yes."

He shook my hand. "My name is Ed Fry. Nice to have you with us."

Any member who had never met Ed Fry missed getting to know the nicest person to ever belong to the fire department.

Fall had set in, and the weather was getting colder. I would go to the firehouse on the second or third Wednesday of the month whenever the company had a meeting or drill. One of these nights, I met Venard Brooks. Venard was still in high school, but he was always buffing around the firehouse, talking about joining the Rescue Company the minute he turned eighteen. Venard's father was a lieutenant in Brooklyn's Rescue 2 and was also Lieutenant Richard Hamilton's chauffer. (Lieutenant Hamilton authored the book *Twenty Thousand Alarms*.) I told Venard that my father was a battalion chief in the Thirty-First Battalion, which was not far from Rescue 2 and that, as a matter of fact, he had responded to quite a few fires and emergencies with Rescue 2. Venard and I would be exchanging our fathers' stories a lot after that.

Sunday mornings were another good time to go the firehouse. I would go to get to know the guys more. One such Sunday morning, a fireman from the Alert Company named Marc Krauss tapped me on the shoulder.

When I looked at him, he asked, "What is your name again?"

"Dan McVey," I replied.

He asked me to go to Arp's Bar to have a few beers, and I accepted his invitation. At the bar, when I pulled money out of my pocket to pay for my beer, he said, "Put that money away. Your money is no good here." Then he paid for my beer.

I was just starting my first beer when Marc was on his second. He talked about the department with me and told me what to expect at fires. Marc belonged to the Alert Engine Company, though, and I was interested in Rescue, which specialized in medical emergencies. So he told me I should try to get into the Engine or Ladder Company and get my EMT certification first, helping out Rescue during the day.

"If you want firefighting experience," he said, "you'll need to join a firefighting company."

He was right. Rescue offered only limited chances to get into fires, as its primary responsibility was to attend to medical emergencies. Firefighting was not out of the question, but it was a secondary role. On the other hand, Rescue offered one of the best fields of experience for people pursuing careers in the medical field.

When I finally made Rescue, Marc would tease me to no end. One minute, he would call us the Band-Aid Brigade, and the next minute he would call the rescue truck a bread truck. That latter joke hit below the belt, however, because, as I said, the rescue truck had been my favorite truck since I'd been a kid.

Rescue was the busiest company in the department. At that time, the company had to respond to every single alarm that came over, for fires as well as for medical emergencies. There was a lot of talk, however, about eliminating Rescue from station calls—those calls for fires that occurred outside and away from dwellings, for example grass fires or car fires—since only one engine company was needed for such situations.

In October, Fire Prevention Week was a cause for big celebration for fire departments all over the country. In our station, there was a big display of posters drawn by grammar school children. And upstairs in the Village Hall, the Rescue Company had their annual pancake breakfast. That morning, I went upstairs to see the guys and asked how much longer it would be before I got sworn in.

Paul Abbruzzese said, "Don't hold your breath until January."

Soon after, I had my fingerprints taken by Police Dispatcher Kenny Fairben. He was a member of the Reliance Engine Company and also Chief Jim Fairben's brother. I had my medical examination around the same time. I also started the EMT course at C. W. Post College. Warden Ralph Gode was an EMT instructor. He worked for the New York State Health Department and had helped me get signed up for the course.

In December, I learned from Chief Ron Nahas that my medical examination was successful, and by that time I already knew that my fingerprints had been approved. Ed Fry and Ralph Gode were standing by.

Ed shook my hand. "Well, that brings you on board my friend."

The second Sunday of that month, the Alert Engine Company was having its children's Christmas party, where Marc introduced me to John Perry. John was a cop assigned to the Manhattan South Task Force. When he heard that I was studying Police Science in college, he tried to discourage me from becoming a cop. At that time, he did not like his job and warned me about what I might be getting myself into. He wanted to get his twenty years in, just so he could get out. However, later on in his career, he was promoted to detective and assigned to the Intelligence Division. He then had a better outlook on his career and decided to do about thirty-something years before retiring.

It was early afternoon when the kid's party ended, and John, Marc, and I went down to Arp's to have a few beers. John continued trying to discourage me from getting into law enforcement, telling me about his own story. He had wanted to be a fireman in the city, but then ended up being a cop. He suggested that I try out for the city fire department instead. We sat and chatted for a while and then went home.

Later that evening, after my family's routine early Sunday dinner, Marc stopped by my house and met my father for the first time.

He shook my father's hand and said, "Hi, Chief." From that point on, he loved to come to my house to listen to my father talk about his war stories as a city firefighter.

After their conversation, Marc and I went back to Arp's to see Pete Gilhooley, who was the evening bartender. Marc's father, ex-Chief Hank Krauss, walked in and sat next to us. He had served as chief of the Floral Park Fire Department in 1975. That night, Hank mentioned something that I remembered throughout my life as a firefighter EMT. He said that you should try not to lose your cool in a fire or an emergency, but use the confidence that you learned at school and in drills, and just get the job done.

Marc and I left Arp's and went to another bar in the Village of Williston Park where I had a few more drinks and a sausage-and-pepper hero. After leaving, we went to the Irish Pub on Hillside Avenue, also in Williston Park. Sitting at the bar, we met a man who had retired from the British army. By this time, we were really starting to feel our drinks and wanted to go home, but this guy wouldn't let us.

"Get these two firemen a beer," he said to the bartender.

We drank the beer and tried to leave.

"Get these two firemen a shot," he said again to the bartender.

We needed a shot like a hole in the head. We were floating enough as it was. I tried to pour the shot on the floor to make it look like I drank it, but this son-of-a-bitch didn't miss a trick.

He said, "Now don't spill it. I'm watching you. We're going to get you drunk tonight."

I didn't know what he was talking about. We were stewed to the hat as it was. We drank the last shot and finally left.

One advantage I had was that I didn't have to get up early the next morning because I didn't have classes on Mondays that semester. Still, I did pay the price the next day. Marc told me later he remembered me saying, "Never again."

I spent my Christmas vacation at my sister's house in Michigan. On Christmas Eve, my brother-in-law's brother, Ray, and I were down in the basement. I don't know how many different types of liquor we tried. You name it; we tried it. By the end of the night, we were quite drunk. I remember it was after midnight. We went upstairs to open presents. My sister gave me a record. It was Ann Murray's *Let's Keep It That Way*.

Before January came, I was back in New York, and I celebrated the New Year with friends. By this time, I knew I was to be introduced into the Rescue Company on January 3, 1979, when the company was to have its monthly meeting. That meeting was my first official company meeting as a member. I was given my plectron—the radio that dispatched us to calls from our homes.

After the meeting, I met Chief Jim Fairben and his lady friend Liz.

Jim asked, "Do you know how to set that sucker up?" (He was referring to my plectron.)

"You plug the wire into the wall," I said, holding up one wire. And then pulling at a second wire, I said, "And this wire is like an antenna."

Jim bought me a mug of beer and gave me a toast. "Good luck, and nice to have you with us."

John Gehrring then joined us, and Jim went on to tell Liz and me that when he'd started in the fire department, John Gehrring had been the captain. John then put his arm around Jim and said, "If there is anything I can do, I will gladly help you." Jim couldn't believe that then, in 1979, he was one rank above John. John had been the next chief in line after Jim.

On the eighth of that month, I appeared before the Fire Council. The chief of the department was Ron Nahas. The first assistant chief was Jim Fairben, and the second assistant chief was John Gehrring. The third assistant chief was John Billerdello. The fourth assistant chief, also known as the baby chief, was Ken Lynch. Warden Ed Fry swore me in. (Wardens are to represent their respective companies at council meetings.) I still was not allowed to respond to calls until my application passed the Village Board.

Shortly thereafter, I went to Florida to see my other sister. By the time I returned to New York, Ricky Maickels told me that I could start responding to calls. He told me to use caution and not to try to be the first one to get there. This made sense because I had absolutely no experience.

Paul Abbruzzese reaffirmed Maickel's advice, telling me, "None of this hero shit."

Therefore, I was careful not to do anything stupid by trying to be a hotshot. Being new, I was going to get in enough trouble without looking for it.

Ed Rothenberg's word of wisdom was that, later on, when people would ask me how many lives I had saved in my job, I would find that I'd lose count. Eventually, I would get the chance to make my first save with Ed.

To start, Active Engine Captain George Funke invited me to ride with his company to fire calls since I lived just across the street from its quarters. I experimented with this suggestion. But it turned out that, by responding with the Active Engine Company, I wasn't gearing up on my own truck on the way to the call, and hence I wasn't getting enough experience responding to fires. So eventually, it was determined that I would be better off driving my car to the main firehouse, where my own company was stationed, to respond with them.

Burning Desires

It was the night of the February council meeting. Pete Feehan was sworn into the Rescue Company. Robert Lofarro was sworn into the Reliance Engine Company. Kevin Green was sworn into the Alert Engine Company either that night or at the previous month's meeting, when I had been sworn in.

This night, however, Pete was in the Rescue room filling out paperwork. Meanwhile, as most newcomers did, we were talking about the abuses we Probationary members knew we were about to face. Pete was already receiving a hard time from the other members, since his father was the village clerk and there was friction between the village political arena and the fire department regarding the ambulance we were going to get. Meanwhile, the town had only a heavy-duty rescue truck that transported victims in critical condition or members of the fire department or their families. In all other cases, the county police ambulance was used to transport patients to the hospital. I knew it was just a matter of time before other members started abusing me since I was one of the new boys on the block. I later found out that it would be like walking on eggs to get approval and acceptance from them.

I was still waiting for my first call. One night I was on Jericho Turnpike. buying a pack of cigarettes. The horn alarm system did not sound because it was after 11:00 at night. However, I heard the siren of the rescue truck from a distance. I knew we had a call. I responded to the firehouse. The black board in front of the firehouse gave the location and I responded. By the time I arrived at the scene, the Nassau County police ambulance was already there. They were carrying the patient on a stair chair. Gary Krug was holding an emesis basin while the patient was vomiting. I knew this was something I had to get used to. I was confident that I would get used to it in a matter of time. Mike Ostipwko told me he was suffering from a hiatus hernia. I said, "That is not life threatening, is it." Mike said "No but it can scare the hell out of you." A hiatus hernia often has the symptoms of a heart attack. This patient was removed to the hospital by the police ambulance. This was the first call I responded to. I knew I had a lot to learn and I had to get used to facing people who are sick or injured. I was determined to develop enough confidence to do just that.

By this time, I was starting the spring semester of my junior year at New York Institute of Technology in Old Westbury. I was at home, doing homework, when I heard the alarm horn sound. It was a 22, which meant a rescue call. Then I heard my radio sound, after which it gave the location and the nature of the emergency: a woman was paralyzed. I ran downstairs, out the door, and to my car. On my way there, I was stopped at a red light on Carnation Avenue and feeling anxious. I remembered what people had said about speeding to the scene and trying to be a hero, however, so I waited. I saw the reflection of the rescue-truck lights shining on the building across the street from the firehouse. They were waiting for the full crew. Finally, they pulled away, sounding the siren, and off they went to the scene. I knew it would be better to miss the truck than to violate traffic rules, so I drove my car to the scene.

When I arrived, I walked into the house. This was the first time I had gone into a house that we had been called to. On the previous call, I had arrived when they were carrying the patient out to the ambulance. Inside the house, I observed an elderly woman lying on the floor, with a cane next to her. She was in a semiconscious state. The men from the company were putting the scoop stretcher under her and splinting her leg.

When they snapped the scoop stretcher, she cried, "I'm dead!"

Jim McEntee said, "No, you're going to be all right."

The Nassau County Police ambulance transported her to the hospital.

Meanwhile, I was shivering due to a combination of the cold weather and the excitement of the call. The crew had acted very professionally, and I knew that this was the way I would have to act if I were to be the one doing the work.

After the call, I was told that she might have had a stroke and that they had splinted her leg and spine to treat for the worst, since she apparently had fallen. The splinting was also done for "psychological first-aid" purposes. The splinting was to make her think that she was not having a stroke.

It was good to talk about calls when they were over so we would all know what to do the next time we ran into a call with similar circumstances; John Bennett had always stressed that idea with me while I was in my first year. Noel Beebe was the captain at that time and had told me that John was very good like that, for training purposes.

We were back in the chief's office when we heard the sirens go off again.

"That's us," Chief Nahas said.

John said, "Okay, I'll drive."

This was my first time responding to a call in the rescue truck. The scene of the emergency was on the north side of town. It was a woman in her sixties who had injured her arm. We splinted her arm and took her vital signs. It was standard procedure to take the pulse, respiration rate, and blood pressure. Her vitals were stable, so she refused transportation to the hospital by ambulance and had her son drive her by private auto.

I recognized her son from the village swimming pool. He was a friend of Ronnie Walsh, the crossing guard. I had helped Ronnie out a few times by taking her to the doctor for routine appointments. Once, I had taken her and her daughter to the doctor's when her daughter had broken her arm. Sometime later, Ronnie and I ran into this patient's son at Roy Rogers on the turnpike, and Ronnie told him that I was good at helping her in crisis.

The man said, "Yes, he helped me out when I was in a crisis. My mother injured her arm and he showed up with the Rescue Company."

It felt good to hear such praise. At meetings, we would get thank-you cards and read notices of thanks published in the local newspaper.

Another night while doing homework in my room, the radio went off. This time it was a woman passed out in a restaurant on Jericho Turnpike. My first impression was that it could be a cardiac arrest. I drove to the firehouse and made the truck. Terry Carney was the driver. When we pulled up to the scene, I still did not know what we were getting into. I was relieved to see that the woman was conscious and breathing, sitting in a chair. She was suffering from an allergic reaction to eating shellfish. We carried her to the rescue truck in the stair chair. We hooked her up to an electrocardiogram in the back of the truck, and she remained stable.

All she kept saying was, "I had such a good dinner and now this has to happen!" At least, she was feeling better, which made me feel better. I guess I felt a sense of relief that it was not a cardiac arrest. But then, that also meant I was still waiting for my first cardiac arrest—something I was not looking forward to at the time. I still needed to build up my confidence for such an event. Little did I know that the only way to get to do was to face the event when it came.

One day after classes, I was at the firehouse when a call came over and the horns sounded. It was an unknown need for aid, per the message over the radio. I was in the rear of the rescue truck waiting for a crew. I was kind of nervous. Pete Walters arrived, entered the rear compartment of the truck, placed a pillow on the bunk, and lay down. I guessed this was just second nature to him.

As we pulled up to the scene, Pete got up from the bunk and pointed to the trauma kit and the resuscitator. "Take that and that," he told me.

Ex-Chief Robert Meehan was outside the house awaiting our arrival. He said we didn't need the resuscitator, because the patient was conscious and breathing. So we brought only the inhalator and the stair chair, since the patient was upstairs. Of course, again, I was relieved that it was not a cardiac arrest. Paul Abbruzzese was upstairs reassuring the patient. I was given the book and told to get the patient information from the police officer.

While I was writing down the information, Sergeant Robert Wagner asked me, "Are you in Rescue now?"

I answered affirmatively.

"That's nice. You will be always helping people in there," he replied.

I had known Sergeant Wagner since I was fourteen years old. I'd seen him a lot at the local swimming pool in the summers. Now he and I would see each other on all of these fire and rescue calls.

Meanwhile, the police ambulance removed the woman to the hospital. I was later to learn that this was a routine call; the woman had been suffering from pulmonary edema, a condition in which the lungs fill up with fluids. I found out a day or two later that she had expired in the hospital.

One cold snowy night, I was hanging out in the firehouse, when a call came over: a possible stroke in the hillcrest section. We already had a crew, so I picked up the police phone and said Rescue would respond.

The cop on the other end said, "Okay. Drive carefully, because it's bad out there."

Off we went, with the siren sounding. The crew and I were in the back of the rescue truck, and Steve Kelly was the driver. Fourth Assistant Chief Kenneth Lynch was riding shotgun. While en route to the scene, I remember praying that I would do my best. I was thinking of Hank Krauss saying, "Don't lose your cool. Just put your knowledge to work and pitch in." I was looking forward into the cab, at the back of Chief Lynch's head. He had gray hair, combed back with no part, which is why he was nicknamed Silver Fox. I saw how relaxed he and the other guys were, and I knew this was how I had to be too. I had the oxygen and the trauma kit ready to go.

As we pulled up to the scene, John Bennett was running out of the house and waving his hands in a downward motion. That meant everything was under control and the patient was stable. I brought the equipment into the house and, there, observed a more experienced newcomer, Tom Koskey. He was fixing the bedclothes, preparing the patient to be transferred from her bed onto a stretcher for when the ambulance arrived. Since there was enough manpower in the house, the rest of us were told to wait outside.

Steve Kelly said, "There is not much you can do for a stroke. Just give oxygen and start an IV." I could give oxygen but an advanced EMT would have to administer drugs. I could not play with that ball until later on.

When the police ambulance arrived, I helped carry the trundle into the house. The cops were in another room talking about a police shooting somewhere in Nassau County. No cops had been hurt, but the suspects had been shot. I remember one cop saying, "The bad guys lost. That's good."

Tom Koskey helped package the patient onto the trundle, and I helped carry her out to the ambulance. From there, she was removed to the hospital.

There was something distinguished about Tom Koskey. He was a real pro at this. So I began helping him do cleanups on the truck, asking him questions. He helped me by answering them and showing me how to use equipment, which some of the other guys wouldn't do. There was a lot of competition for glory, I guess.

Another more experienced newcomer was Gary Krug. He was a registered nurse. He had about a year in the department, as did Tom. I had met Gary while shopping on Tulip Avenue, at which point he'd said, "If there is anything I can do to help you, just let me know. I know that some of these guys enjoy keeping their knowledge away from others. I try not to do that."

The next time I met Gary Krug, he gave me a list of basic procedures to follow when approaching a patient. "Here, look this over when you're not busy," he told me. "This will help you get your feet wet."

The list included questions that I should ask patients, such as "Are you on medication?" and "Are you under a doctor's care?" along with basic steps that I had observed other members taking while we were on calls. But it gave me an idea of what to do if I were ever the first one on a scene.

One night, about two or three in the morning, I was asleep at home when a general alarm came over the radio. It was a garage fire. I ran from my house to the firehouse across the street, and used the active company truck for transportation. While en route to the scene, the guys were talking about the nature of the call. We knew it was something big. I was sitting in the jump seat looking at the guys gearing up on the hose bed. I remember Joe Oswald buckling up his turnout coat, and the mars lights flashing in his face. Turning on the road after the Floral Park Railroad Station, Tyson Avenue, the floodlight truck had its siren whining. Then as we turned onto Jericho Turnpike, I looked through the front cab window and saw the garage fire, already in full swing. I left the Engine Company, reported to Rescue, and put on my turnout gear. Shortly thereafter, the fire was quickly under control. The only job left for the Rescue Company was to make a first-aid station. Nobody was injured as far as I can remember. I also remember trying to talk to one of our firefighters, and he just turned and walked away very slowly without saying a word. This kind of behavior was what made people from other companies think we were a bunch of snobs. From the time I had submitted my application, I had heard people talking negatively about Rescue. I think some of it was jealousy, but some of it was true. I didn't know. I was just trying to do the right thing. I was making my averages and I was enrolled in an EMT course.

It was around this time that I was to do my emergency-room observation training. I had a lot to learn yet, and I was just hoping that I would get the chance to overcome my inexperience. My EMT instructor gave us a form to document all our time in the ER. We had to do eight hours. We could document time in any ER, but he advised us to go to the hospital where we would take most of our patients. The hospital our company used the most was Nassau Hospital in Mineola, so I reported there. I went to the waiting room and spoke to the head nurse. Then I waited for about twenty minutes, after which she called me into the emergency room. She showed me all of the treatment rooms and explained how they put patients in different rooms based on the nature of their medical problems. She encouraged me to ask questions, but I was still so green in the medical field, the only way I was going to break the ice was to just do it. We arranged my schedule. I would be doing two days in a row, with four hours each day. Tomorrow was to be my first day.

The next day, I reported to the emergency room. The same head nurse told me to stand by the door where the ambulance crews wheeled in patients. So I did, and waited for further instruction.

About five minutes later, she called me to the reception desk where she was seated and said sarcastically, "You can just stand there and watch the ambulances, or you can try to learn something by walking around and observing."

So I walked from room to room. Eventually, the Floral Park Rescue team brought in an overdose case. When I saw the truck backing up, I knew it had to be serious, because our truck didn't transport unless it was a matter of life or death. Terry Carney told the attending nurse that it was an overdose—in fact, it was the typical overdose behind Lee's Drug Store on a Saturday night. Our guys wheeled in the patient, who was in a semiconscious state. His eyes were sunken and lackluster. Mike Ostipwko said that my average was going to hell; they must have had a few calls while I had been out of town.

They wheeled the patient into the trauma room. One doctor put a gastric tube up his nose, and the patient started to violently gag. I saw the stomach contents travel up the clear, colorless tube. Another doctor took a syringe, "vacuumed" up the vomit, and put it into a jar. As the patient continued violently gagging and thrashing about, I started to feel nausea. I walked out of the room and out of the emergency entrance for some fresh air. This was my worst nightmare. Every member of Rescue had the same fear when first starting—they worried about getting sick on a call. And some did. One member responded to a DOA and vomited on the body. Another time, when a cardiac arrest victim vomited all over the ceiling of the truck, about five or six of the guys stuck their heads out a window and heaved while the patient's vomit dripped from their heads. I never did vomit on a call, but I thought I was going to on this particular night.

I went back to the trauma room, and they were still pumping out the victim's stomach. I was still unable to face the scene, so I went back out into the hallway for more air.

The head nurse came out and said, "If you want to stand by the door and watch the ambulances, that's fine. But I would suggest you go inside for the experience."

When I returned, they were done pumping the patient's stomach, and a nurse was telling him how stupid he had been for doing what he had. She then told me that if they had not started an IV and pumped him, he would have died. Feeling better now, I helped her move the patient to the Intensive Care Unit on another floor. I was still ashamed that I hadn't been able to face the scene the way I should have, but then I was thinking that I had been the only person who had ever felt this way.

The next day, I was at the firehouse talking about the incident, and Mike Ostipwko said, "Yes, they stick the tube right up the nose and right into the stomach."

I admitted my stomach weakness, and Ex-Chief Hank Krauss said, "That'll teach you not to use drugs."

Later on, we were dispatched to the church across the street. The call came over as "A lady is not feeling well," To which ex-Captain Rickie Maickels said, "I know she's not feeling well. Otherwise we wouldn't be called out."

We arrived within seconds. This call was a nightmare, because the patient was conscious but in a weakened condition, and she didn't want to go to the hospital. With her husband trailing behind, we put her in the truck and hooked her up to the EKG. I don't know how good or how bad the EKG reading was, because I was not yet advanced enough in my EMT training to know how to read EKGs, but what I did know was that the other men were trying to talk her into going to the hospital, since, apparently, she needed to. It was at that point that her husband collapsed into the arms of Pete Walter.

Pete yelled, "Stair chair!"

I ran out with the stair chair and they put the patient's husband on it. He immediately regained consciousness and said, "She doesn't want to go."

The law says that if a patient is conscious and in a sound state of mind, that patient has the right to refuse to go to the hospital. We could not force her to go. However, since her husband became a patient, we had the authority to take him to the hospital. Therefore, they both went for the ride. I did not go on the ride to the hospital in this case, but I found out later that both the husband and wife were admitted and then released.

Finally, we got a call for a possible cardiac arrest. I recognized the address of the emergency as Police Officer Robert Gallo's. I'd known Bob Gallo since I was eight. I responded to the scene by way of the truck, concerned that it could be him. When we arrived, however, I saw him in uniform in front of his house. And as I brought the equipment into the house, I learned that it was his father-in-law who was suffering from chest pains. We administered oxygen and then transported him to Nassau Hospital.

This had been the first call that Bob had seen me on, so he said, "Look at this. He is in Rescue now!" He'd always liked to kid around with me.

Later on that night, I went to Nassau Hospital for my last four hours of emergency room training. I went to the treatment room where we'd had the overdose the night before. As fate would have it, I saw Bob Gallo sitting by his father-in-law, drinking a cup of coffee. I told him this was the room where we'd brought the overdose.

"I was the one who sent that call in," he said. "I chased a bunch of kids from behind Lee's Drug Store and he collapsed in front of me."

"That really got to me when they pumped his stomach out," I told him.

"You get used to it," he said. "When I was a rookie, my first DOA was a woman who died in the bathtub. Her feces were expelled and the stench made me puke. Another time I was called for a man run over by a train and the same thing. I puked."

Earlier that day, another guy from the company had also told me I would see worse. He said that once, when he was new, he'd walked into a house for a call that had come over as a cardiac. The cop had told him not to go in, but he went anyway, hoping the patient might still be saved with CPR. He got to the room where the man was only to see a double-gauge shotgun at his feet and brain matter literally splattered all over the ceiling. Another time, he'd seen a man who'd been fatally hit by a train. On the tracks was an amputated foot with the sneaker still on it. He didn't vomit but admitted his stomach turned and said he dry-heaved. After that, he began wondering whether Rescue was the right company for him, but stuck it out and stayed anyway.

After my earlier experience, these words of wisdom, from Bob Gallo and other Rescue personnel, gave me encouragement.

Back in the ER, across the hall from where Bob and I were, there was a DOA in one treatment room and, in another, a person with a deep cut on his thumb. While I was observing in those two rooms, the doctor gave Bob's father-in-law a clean bill of health. The tests had come back negative—it was not a heart attack. Meanwhile, the father-in-law was flirting with the nurse in his room.

The nurse would ask him, "How do you feel?" to which he'd reply, "When I see you, I feel great." At that time, Bob and his father-in-law were discharged from the hospital.

The nurse then came up to me and told me to watch to make sure nobody was looking, because she was going to wheel the DOA patient to a nearby shower room. The coast was clear, so she put the corpse in the shower room. An hour later, an orderly arrived to remove the body. He opened the door to the shower room and the body was exposed. Her hands and feet were tied up and she was in a frog position. She was naked and the color of blueberry yogurt. There was a horrible stink, like rotten eggs, or perhaps worse.

"Oh no," I said to myself, "Here we go again." I tried to hide in an empty treatment room, but a nurse followed me and said, "Oh, come on. Face it and get your feet wet."

At least she was nicer about it than the head nurse had been. This one spoke in a kidding-around way. So I came back out of the treatment room. The door to the shower room was closed with the body still inside. The orderly was sitting in a chair, white as a ghost, with sweat forming on his forehead.

"I thought I had a strong stomach when it came to this," he said.

"Oh, come here," the nurse said and wiped his forehead like a mother would do for her child.

I said, "Don't feel bad. I saw an OD get his stomach pumped last night and I thought I was going to shoot my cookies." His reaction made me feel that I wasn't the only one with this kind of problem.

The rest of the night, there were but a few routine emergencies. One person had appendicitis, a few had stomach viruses, and a fifteen-year-old girl had been hit by a car. I also saw a few cuts that needed stitching and a fractured leg. At the time, I didn't feel I was getting anything out of the experience. But later on, I never regretted it, because it was the start of my experience. It was now or never that I had to try, and then to make today's failures tomorrow's successes.

Another memorable time that February was the first-aid tournament at the Our Lady of Victory School gym. I remember riding back and forth in the passenger seat of the rescue truck, while John Bennett drove us from the firehouse to the school and back. We were taking equipment out to the school and setting it up for the tournament, along with food for a reception afterward.

As we were turning the last corner before reaching the school, he asked, "How are you enjoying the Rescue Company?"

I replied, "I like it. I'm like a kid with a new toy."

Ex-Captain Ed Fry was conducting the tournament. He would yell out what was happening to a patient, for example, "The patient is bleeding from the left arm!" or "The patient just went into cardiac arrest!" and then the contestants had to react accordingly.

There were a lot of female EMTs from different volunteer ambulance corps there. The Floral Park Fire Department didn't have any female members until 1983.

Lieutenant Garry Gronert, knowing I was single, told me, "You can get a lot of nice young women here."

I flirted with one or two of them, but never got a date.

John Bennett told me later that the first-aid team would be a good group for me to join. "You will be constantly bandaging and splinting, and you will become good at it," he said.

Unfortunately, the first-aid team of the Floral Park Rescue Company disbanded shortly after that tournament, so I never had the opportunity.

The day after the first-aid tournament, I was awakened by a fire alarm at home. The call came over as a garage fire. After the radio message was broadcasted, the audio alarm system sounded what's called "a 77," which meant every company must respond. I quickly dressed and ran downstairs to leave out of the side door. To my surprise there were about three or four feet of snow on the ground. I pulled my boots up and trudged across the street through the deep snow to the Active Firehouse. I sat in the jump seat, while the guys from the Engine Company suited up.

We arrived at the scene about three minutes later. I went to the rescue truck to suit up. After the fire was extinguished, most units were put on a Signal 13, which meant, "Return to your quarters." The Active Company was one of the units signaled, but the Rescue Company wasn't. Therefore, Active had to leave without me. When all units were ready, the chief put us all on a 13, and I got a ride back home in the rescue truck. Before being dropped off, I was asked if

I was available to do a snow standby. I said I would but only after I shoveled the snow from my house. I shoveled the snow as quickly as I could and then walked a half a mile to the main firehouse, where my company was stationed.

At the firehouse, we did a lot of work cleaning up the rescue company room. Captain Beebe thought it would be a good idea to do so since we had the manpower. Afterward, we all went upstairs to have lunch. They were making hamburgers.

Right in the middle of lunch, we were banged out on a call: a child with convulsions. We all ran downstairs, piled onto the truck, and raced to the scene on the north side of town. Once there, John Bennett ran into the house and, less than a half-minute later, came back out carrying the child in his arms. He brought the boy onto the back of the truck. The mother was with him and also got on. The doors of the truck closed and Rickie Maickels, the driver, yelled out to the back, "Is everyone ready to go?"

"Yes!" John Bennett yelled up. Then off we went to the hospital.

By this time, most of the snow had been cleared from the streets so we were all allowed to go home and respond to calls from there.

BUS FIRE

IT WAS THE BEGINNING OF March and the winter of 1979 was coming to a close. However, it was still kind of cold. We had just been called out to a bus fire at a bus company on Jericho Turnpike, and we were in the back of the truck suiting up for the call. Captain Noel Beebe was in the passenger seat in the cab, with the radiotelephone pressed to his ear.

He yelled back to us "Signal Ten!" That is when we knew it was a working fire.

When we pulled up to the scene, black smoke was bellowing out of a bus. We set up a first-aid station in preparation for any injuries that may occur during the extinguishment process. I don't remember any firefighters being hurt on this run; however, Chief Jim Fairben called us to the bus company's main building for possible aid to one of the workers. When I arrived inside, I saw Chief Fairben standing next to the patient as oxygen was being administered to him. At this point, the patient seemed stable, but Chief Fairben advised him to go to the hospital anyway as a precaution. The patient was a diabetic, which is not good when accompanied by smoke inhalation. The patient did not want to go to the hospital, however, so signed the form releasing us from the scene.

Chief Fairben asked him, "Are you sure you don't want to go to the hospital?"

The guy insisted that he did not want to go.

"If you get me out of bed tonight," the chief told him, "I'm going to kick your ass all the way to the hospital."

We were released from the scene and went back to the firehouse. Chief Fairben predicted that we would be back for this guy because we'd already seen him another time prior to this incident.

Back at the firehouse, I was in the Rescue room and Chief Fairben was in the Hook and Ladder room. He had decided to hang out for a while because he knew we would get banged out for a rescue call back at the bus company. Sure enough, about ten minutes later, the police were dispatched and then the radio sounded for a rescue call back to the bus company. I exited the Rescue room and walked past the Hook room to see Chief Fairben with a disgusted look on his face.

"You were right," I said. "We're going back to that clown."

"That son-of-a-bitch," the chief said. "I told him he should go to the hospital." Chief Fairben sped off to the scene in his car, ahead of the rescue truck. A crew promptly piled on the truck, and off we went.

As we pulled up to the scene, Chief Fairben exclaimed, "Get the stair chair! We're transporting!"

The way he had ordered the stair chair and transportation meant this was serious. I walked into the building that I had walked out of just awhile earlier and saw the same patient on oxygen, in a semiconscious state of distress. The guy could not talk, so he nodded or shook his head in response to our questions. We put him in back of the truck, still on oxygen, and hooked him up to the telemetry (a type of cardiac monitor). Someone asked him if he had any chest pain and he nodded.

Then Kevin Tholl asked him, "Do you feel like you're going to puke?" He shook his head.

We transported him to Nassau Hospital, where he was admitted.

A few months later or so, I mentioned the incident again to Jim Fairben, and he said that the patient had died as a result of diabetic complications.

A Returned Favor

For a couple of years before entering the department, I did a lot of favors for Ronnie Walsh and Fran Donlon. I took Ronnie to doctor's appointments when her husband was not home. I drove Fran to a storefront a few times to help her sell chances for the church. I drove them both to and from the village swimming pool on many occasions. Several times, they both said that they didn't know how to thank me for driving them around whenever they didn't have rides.

One very cold, wintry day, I had sent my car to the mechanic for a repair job. If I remember correctly, it was to fix an oil leak in the engine. My car was done and ready to be picked up, but my father wasn't home to drive me to the shop. I wasn't about to walk to the shop because it was too cold. I thought about Ronnie and Fran. I figured that one of them would hook me up with a ride, since they each owed me one. I knew Ronnie more than I knew Fran, so I called her first. The phone rang two or three times and then she answered.

"Mrs. Walsh, is your husband home?" I asked.

She said, "No baby, what's the matter?"

"Well, I have to get my car at the shop and it's too cold to walk."

"Oh my God, he's not home," she said. "You know if I could, I would be there in a minute. Oh, Danny, I feel so bad I can't help."

"I know," I said. "I'll call Mrs. Donlon. She owes me one."

"I'm sure she can do it. She drives, and they have more than one car."

"Okay, I'll call her or someone else."

"I'm sorry, Danny," she said again. "You know I would be there if I could."

"Don't worry. I can get either Mrs. Donlon or someone else to take me." I wasn't too surprised by Ronnie's response, as I had figured her husband was at work.

After we hung up, I called Mrs. Donlon. Mrs. Donlon was a native of Ireland and spoke with an accent. She was also very religious. You name it, she did it for the church: she was a Eucharistic minister, she sold chances at storefronts, and she worked in the rectory toward the end of her time, just before she passed away.

"Hello, Mrs. Donlon." I said when she answered.

"Hello, Danny love. What can I do for you?"

"Can you drive me to the shop to pick up my car? It's kind of cold to be walking."

She said, with no hesitation, "Sure, Danny love. I'll be right over." I gave her directions to my house and we hung up. I was relieved to know that I had a ride.

While I was waiting for her to pick me up, a rescue call came in. A woman had fallen down the stairs on Oak Street. I was still too eager at that point in my career to miss a call, so I thought I would ask Fran to drive me to the call and then I could get one of the firemen to drive me to the shop afterward. I left my house and walked down the block toward Atlantic Avenue. From a distance, I observed a very slow-moving car. It was traveling about fifteen miles an hour in a thirty-mile-an-hour zone. An impatient motorist sped around the slow car and blew his horn in an impatient rage. The slow vehicle then turned on its left blinker and rounded the corner onto the street where I lived. Sure enough, it was Fran.

I jumped into her car. "There is a rescue call on Oak Street. Would it be a problem if you took me to the call, and I can get one of the firemen to take me to the service station?"

"Sure, honey," she replied. "I'll take you to Oak Street."

At that point, she put the pedal to the floor and sped away, leaving tire marks on the road. She went from about fifteen miles an hour to a good sixty miles an hour down the main residential street.

While I was trying to put on my seatbelt, she made a sharp right turn on Carnation Avenue. As soon as we heard the siren of the rescue truck, she slowed up to let the truck make a left turn in front of us. Then, with the truck driving in front of us, she picked up a little more speed. She ran a red light on Plainfield Avenue. Horns were honking from the cross traffic. Finally, we arrived at the call without an accident. I don't remember whether the patient went to the hospital, but I think it was a refusal, after which we were released from the scene. Paul Dombrowski drove me to the service station to pick up my car.

HE'S OUR BROTHER

IN THE NEW YORK CITY Fire Department, a Probationary Firefighter is considered either a white cloud or a black cloud. The black cloud is a person who gets all of the big fires and emergencies. Whenever this type of probie is around, there seems to be a big job. On the other hand, when the white cloud is around, everything seems quiet. It sometimes takes a few months for the white cloud to get his big job. I was, what I would call, a black cloud when it came to fires. During my first few months, I saw some good ones. However, when it came to big aid cases, such as cardiac arrests, I was a very white cloud.

It wasn't until sometime in April 1979 that a call came over for a cardiac-related illness. The patient was conscious when the police and fire chiefs arrived. Officer Gallo and Sergeant Wagner were the police officers assigned to the scene.

When we arrived in the heavy-duty rescue truck, Chief Gehring met us at the door. I heard him tell the guys in a soft, professional voice, "He's going into arrest."

Carrying a piece of equipment—either the oxygen or the trauma kit—I walked past the kitchen where I saw Father Livoti, the company chaplain, sitting with two women. One of the women said in a soft, emotional voice, "Please help him. He's our brother."

Past the kitchen, on the left, was the bedroom where the patient was. I handed over the piece of equipment and observed Rickie Maickels administering breathing ventilations with his ambu-bag. Paul Dombrowski was doing CPR compressions. I heard an order for the suction unit and immediately ran outside to the truck to get it. Back in the house, I heard the Nassau County Police ambulance approaching, with the siren whining. I was determined to face this and do the best I could, because saving lives was important to me. I went to the room where the patient was and handed over the suction unit. Paul was still doing compressions, and Rickie was wiping vomit off the patient's face with a gauze pad. He then returned to ventilations.

The Nassau cop assigned to the NCPD ambulance walked in and made a quick observation of the scene. He pointed at me and said, "Open the sliding door on the side of my ambulance and get me the wooden box with blue letters on it."

I ran out of the house, found the ambulance, and opened the sliding door. There it was. It was a wooden trauma kit with the blue letters NCPD printed on it. I took the box back into the house and gave it to the cop. He took it and began working on the patient. He then started an IV line and administered drugs through the line. He used sodium bicarb to neutralize acidosis in the blood and epinephrine to try to stimulate the heart. The patient was still not breathing, and there were still no signs of his heart beating.

The cop said, "Get back on him," and then started the one-thousand count to pace the compressions and ventilations: "One-one-thousand, two-one-thousand … " and so on, reaching up to five-one-thousand before returning again to one. Every time he reached five-one-thousand, the person at the head of the patient ventilated the lungs with the ambu-bag.

Finally, they called for the trundle—the stretcher with wheels. Ex-Chief Bobby Meehan and I ran out to the ambulance to get it and carried it back into the room where the patient was. A few minutes later, the patient was on the trundle, and they slowly wheeled him through the kitchen, with CPR still in progress. They had to stop the CPR for a few seconds to carry him down the steps outside the front door, but once they were at the bottom, they resumed the process, with the Nassau cop continuing the one-thousand count. They stopped CPR for a few more seconds to lift the patient up into the ambulance. Two of our firemen were already in the ambulance waiting, and as soon as the patient was wheeled in, these two immediately resumed CPR. Paul Dombrowski, Paul Abbruzzese, and Garry Gronert rode in the back of the ambulance on the way to the hospital.

Captain Noel Beebe called the rest of the crew, which included me, and told us to clean up the room where the patient had been. There were needles on the floor, along with some dirty gauze pads and oxygen equipment. All of this had to be disposed of or cleaned, if reusable. Back at the firehouse, we cleaned all of the reusable equipment and straightened up the back of the rescue truck.

When we were finished, I went to Chief Gehring's office. He was sitting at his desk with a sad expression. "That's too bad about this guy," I said.

"Sixty-two years old," he replied. "It's worse when it's one of your friends."

I sat there and talked to the chief while waiting for the guys to come back from the hospital. I was anxious to see how the patient made out. The way the chief was talking, based on his professional experiences, it sounded as if the patient wasn't going to make it.

The ambulance returned with our three men. They stepped out and shut the sliding door. As the bus left, I went up to Garry. "How did the guy make out?"

"DOA. We got his heart going while we were on the way to the hospital, but he crapped out on us and never came back. We worked on him for a while in the ER, too, but they pronounced him."

Sergeant Wagner drove up just then. "Hey, Mac," he asked. "How did that guy make out?"

I told him, adding, "I feel kind of bad, since this is my first arrest."

"You feel bad?" asked the sergeant. "That's stress. You'll get a lot of that around here."

Then Officer Bob Gallo approached us, and Sergeant Wagner told him, "You know that guy went down? Danny was telling me."

"I know," Gallo said. "They just told me. I was talking to the guy and then I let Rescue take over. I went into the kitchen to take information. Then I heard a thud. I walked back in the bedroom and I saw Noel Beebe doing CPR. He'd seemed okay other then he was having chest pains."

Wagner looked at me and pushed his two fists together. "It feels like a vice."

It was getting late. It was 11:00 and the police were changing shifts.

"I got school tomorrow," I said. "I better get going."

Sergeant Wagner shook my hand. "Goodnight, Mac. Don't take it too hard."

Unknown Difficulty with a Baby

It was an ordinary Sunday afternoon. I was home on a regular day off from school when a call came over as an "unknown difficulty with a baby." The location of the call was around the corner from the main firehouse. It all happened so quickly.

I responded to the scene in my car, and as I approached the address, which was an apartment complex, I saw John Bennett running with a baby in his arms. Running with him was a woman, who I assumed was the baby's mother, and Hugo Berta. They cut through the back of the complex, ran into the adjacent parking lot of the police station, and jumped into the backseat of a police car. At the same time, the baby's mother jumped into the passenger seat of another police car, and Hugo jumped into the backseat of the car that John was in. As sirens began wailing, I observed John performing infant CPR on the baby. I knew this wasn't good. Both police cars left in very little time, and made their way to Long Island Jewish Hospital. All of this happened in just a few minutes. We didn't even wait for a full crew to man the truck.

We went downstairs to the Rescue Company room to wait for Hugo and John to come back. A few minutes later, Ex-Chief Bobby Meehan walked in the room and said, "They just called from the hospital. The baby was DOA."

Later on, I went home and told my mother and father that it was a SIDS. My mother said, "The poor little thing. Are you upset?"

"Not really," I said. "I'm hanging in there. It all happened so fast that I didn't get a chance to get a piece of the action." That is probably why I was not too emotionally involved. I didn't see enough of it to get upset.

They talked about the incident in the firehouse for a few days, and I learned that it was not a SIDS case. The autopsy revealed that the baby died from internal injuries resulting from suspected child abuse. The baby's father was arrested after an investigation.

A Ticket to Eighty-Six

It was after dark. Paul Abbruzzese, Louie Mancuso, and I were doing some work on the rescue truck, replacing supplies and maintaining equipment, when we decided that it would be a good time to go get gas for the truck. I went to the police station to get the key for the gas pump, and then we were on our way to the village garage where the pump was located. Paul was driving, Louie was riding shotgun, and I was in the back. As we were driving down Stewart Street, a call came over. All I heard was "A Signal Nine on East Cherry Street." We never made it to the gas pump. One of the guys turned on the siren and we were on our way to the call.

Louie notified the dispatcher that we were on our way to the scene and told him that all Rescue personnel must respond to the scene and not to the firehouse.

We were about halfway there when Louie yelled back to me, "We have a cardiac arrest!" I quickly set up the resuscitator, turning the oxygen on and plugging the mask into the unit, so it would be ready to use. As we pulled up to the scene, I had the oxygen in my hand and was ready to go. I grabbed the trauma kit with my free hand and ran into the house. We were led to the kitchen, where an eighty-six-year-old man was in cardiac arrest. Hugo Berta was on compressions, and Ronnie Nahas was on ventilations. There was no way I was going to get my hands on this one, since there was too much manpower at this scene. I did help by setting up the Reeves stretcher, but I was still kind of nervous. My knees were shaking.

A police officer put his hand on my shoulder and said, "Are you a relative?"

I said, "No. I'm from Rescue."

The Reeves stretcher is a litter-type stretcher that doesn't have wheels like the trundle, but in this case, we didn't have a trundle available. Therefore, we had to stop CPR for a few seconds to place the patient on the stretcher, resume CPR for a few seconds, and then stop CPR again while carrying him out of the house. Once on the front lawn, we resumed CPR again. A few seconds later, we stopped CPR, carried him to the truck, and resumed CPR on the ground outside the truck. Then we had to stop the CPR a final time to get the patient in the truck and on the bench.

Pete and I were in the back of the truck offering assistance. An Advanced Emergency Medical Technician (AEMT)used the defibrillator on the patient. They resumed CPR after the attempt was unsuccessful. At this point, Pete and I were ordered off of the truck and told to stay in town. After the truck left for the hospital, Pete drove me back to the firehouse. Pete was rather disappointed that we had to stay.

"What do probies like us do?" he said.

We were kind of laid back, and it was hard to get experience during night calls, since they took place when everyone was home from their regular jobs, and were thus heavily manned.

I remained at the firehouse because I wanted to see how they made out with the patient. As the rescue truck pulled up, Chief Ken Lynch jumped out of the passenger seat. I approached him as he was walking toward the chief's office.

He put his ear close to my mouth so he could hear me ask, "How did the guy make out?"

He shook his head. "Dead."

"Ah, shit."

"If God gave me a ticket to eighty-six, I would be satisfied," he said.

I replied, "Well, I guess you can't save everyone."

Installation of 1979

Traditionally, the first Tuesday in April is when all companies have their meetings to elect officers for the year. Each company votes separately for its own officers. Then, at the combined Thursday night meeting the following week, the entire department votes for the chiefs. This was our company's year to elect a new fourth assistant chief, since Ronnie Nahas was leaving the position. Mike Ostipwko went from first lieutenant to captain, John Bennett was elected first lieutenant, and Paul Abbruzzese was elected second lieutenant. Rickie Maickels was chosen to run for the department's fourth assistant chief. The offices of the captain and the two lieutenants were effective immediately after the meeting. However, the office of fourth assistant chief would not go into effect until the following Thursday.

After the Tuesday meeting, we went upstairs to eat. Pete Walters had cooked roast beef and had a whole buffet of food. One thing I will say for Pete is that he sure was a good chef. I sat next to Paul Abbruzzese. He was twenty-three at the time, and he was the company's lieutenant. I was having fun and I wanted to stay, but I had school the next day. I asked Paul if it was all right if I left early, and he said yes since school was more important.

For the next few weeks, many of the guys were talking about whom they were taking to the installation dinner. Once, I remember one of our members on the phone in the chief's room saying, in a frustrated tone, "My love life is not the greatest these days. All I need is a date for the installation dinner!"

He had apparently just been rejected because he slammed the phone down in disgust.

"She said no again?" I heard someone say to him.

I chimed in. "I have nobody to take that night either, so don't feel too bad."

One night, Marc Krauss and I went out to dinner at Easy Street

Café on Tulip Avenue in Franklin Square. We both had brook trout. It was all right. I was not a big fish eater back then. Afterward, we went a few blocks away to the Plattdeutsche Park Restaurant for a few drinks.

We went up to the bar and Marc ordered two beers. When I took out my money to pay, he said, "Put that away. Your money's no good here."

Later, as we sat over our beers, he said, "This is where the installation dinner is next week." We sat and talked for a while and then went home.

On the Thursday night before the installation dinner, the chiefs were sworn in. This was the night that the chiefs officially took office, prepared to take on their responsibilities. Ron Nahas went out as chief. He made his outgoing speech and verbally handed his position over to his first assistant chief, James Fairben. John Gehring remained the first assistant chief, John Billerdello the second assistant chief, and Ken Lynch the third assistant chief. Last but not least, Rickie Maickels became the fourth assistant chief. After the ceremony, the department gathered in the party room to have food, beer, and soda.

On Friday night, the night before the installation dinner, all of the members were assigned to our respective stations to wash and wax the trucks. After this was done, we set the company room up for Tom Koskey's bachelor party. We put a ball and chain on Tom's ankle and made him drink, while we watched silent porno movies. By the end of the night, everyone, especially Tom, was feeling the drinks. Tom made a short speech, thanking us for the party, and invited everyone to his wedding.

While we were cleaning up, I said to Paul Abbruzzese, "This is a bad thing to say, but I feel like going out on a call."

Paul said, "Yes, sometimes you do get that feeling."

Saturday was the installation dinner. At 6:00, the department assembled at headquarters. We lined up and marched around the block, stopping in front of the village hall, where the trucks were lined up with a firefighter standing at attention. The department then lined up and the chief, the fire commissioner, and the mayor performed an inspection of our uniforms and the trucks. Then we were dismissed to go to the installation dinner. Before going, our company lined up in front of the truck for a company picture, and then we all left together.

As I walked into the meeting venue, I recognized it as the place Marc and I had gone after eating at the Easy Street Café. That night, I formally met Ted Bellmonte, although I had known who he was since I was about ten. He was from Engine 2, and this was a special night for Engine 2, because Jim Fairben was from that company, and he was being installed as chief of the department.

After the cocktail hour was over, everyone assembled in the dining hall. My company was seated by the fire exit, which was opened for ventilation, and outside, we could see was the new chief's car. Jim Fairben was the first chief to use this car.

After the opening ceremony, which included the pledge of allegiance, the benediction, and other such traditions, the company officers were lined up to be sworn in. Then the officers were dismissed back to their seats and the chiefs lined up to be sworn in. This was a special night for Rescue, since one of our men, Ron Nahas, was stepping down as chief, and Rickie Maickels was being installed as fourth assistant chief. We had nicknamed Rickie "Moose," so as he was marching up to the line, our guys were singing the Mickey Mouse song, but singing "Mickey Moose" instead of "Mickey Mouse."

After the ceremony came the food and dancing. I went up to the chiefs' table and congratulated all of the new chiefs, and then I went socializing. I met a woman whose husband was a member of the Alert Engine Company. He was not there that night, however, because he was ill. She put her arm around me and gave all kinds of praise to the Rescue Company, telling me about how her husband had once been in cardiac arrest and how the Gronert twins, Garry and Dennis, had saved his life. Dennis was no longer in the company because he had moved out of town.

QUESTIONS, ANSWERS, AND WAR STORIES

ONE THING COMMON TO PEOPLE who work in vital public services—for example, cops, firemen, nurses, and doctors—is war stories. You will always hear these public servants talking about blood, guts, and vomit at the dinner table. Such stories are not only told to entertain the listeners but to give a realistic picture of what these people face.

When I first met Paul Abbruzzese, he told me such a story for the latter reason. He said that it was a lot of work to be in Rescue. That you also had to be a firefighter and that you had to attend fire school in Bethpage. I clearly remember him saying, as he was eating a donut and drinking a cup of coffee, "Scenes of cardiac arrest are not as clean as some might think, with people puking in your mouth."

Back when I still wanted to learn about the profession, though, I searched out such stories. I was told by some that, to learn, I should ask questions, but to be careful whom I asked. As one member told me, "Some people enjoy keeping their knowledge from others." Rescue was kind of competitive in that way. Therefore, I only asked those who *liked* to tell stories.

One member who liked to tell stories was Garry Gronert. He recounted a lot of experiences that made me worry how I would react when faced with something similar. One time, he had an attempted suicide where the person stabbed himself about fourteen times in the throat, cutting both carotid arteries. Garry and his brother Dennis had beat the truck to the scene, and when they were running up to the house, he saw a chief from another company leaning over the stoop railing, vomiting in the bushes. When they saw this, they new there was something very ugly inside the house. They both ran upstairs and saw the patient on a blood-soaked bed. There was blood spurting in all different directions from his throat, and there was coagulated blood all over the floor. Rescuers were trying desperately to control the bleeding by holding a large abdominal pad over the man's throat without choking him. Meanwhile, they were slipping and sliding on the blood that had pooled on the floor. When the truck arrived, they loaded the patient into the back without wasting any time.

To make the situation even more stressful, the patient whispered to Dennis, "Hey you. Come here."

Dennis put his ear next to the guy's mouth to hear the man say in a weak voice, "I swallowed two bottles of pills."

All they could do was administer an IV and tell the hospital about the overdose so they could pump his stomach as well as treat the self-inflicted injuries on his throat. The man miraculously survived.

Garry talked a lot about calls he made with his brother Dennis, who had since left the company because he had moved out of town. Once, Garry said, "That poor guy used to specialize in getting barfed on."

Whenever the two were the first on the scene of a cardiac arrest, Garry told me, he would run ahead of Dennis so he could start CPR compressions and have Dennis do the mouth-to-mouth.

"One day we had someone having the big one," he said. "I ran ahead of Dennis and started the compressions. After awhile, I felt the guy belch. I looked up at Dennis, and the vomit was dripping from his glasses."

I asked Garry, "If the patient starts to vomit, can you pull back in time before it gets in your mouth?"

"Well, once you hear that magic belch, it's too late. Usually by that time the guy's puke is already in the back of your throat."

Sometimes I liked to hear the same story over again, and Garry, a lot of times, loved to tell the same story over. Once, he repeated this story about Dennis's glasses dripping with vomit, and then followed it up with a new one that I hadn't heard.

"One time, my brother and I were the first on the scene where the guy was in cardiac arrest. I ran in and started the compressions and

Dennis started mouth-to-mouth. It turned out that the guy was dead from an aneurysm of the aorta, and a gallon of blood came out of the guy's mouth right into Dennis' face.

"Another time I was stuck doing the mouth-to-mouth and Dennis was on compressions. He ripped open the guy's shirt to begin CPR, and it turned out the patient had a colostomy. Dennis accidentally ripped open the colostomy bag and all of the guy's shit poured all over Dennis' lap."

In a way, I thought the stories were a bit humorous. In another way, I found them intimidating because I knew I would be routinely confronted with similar situations. Garry wasn't only trying to be funny. He was also giving the new guys a realistic picture of what a rescue call was really like.

Like he'd said at the CPR course I took, for which he was an instructor, "Now you can get disgusted and back away, and let someone die, or you can treat that person as if it were one of your own family. We throw up. The patients throw up. We all throw up at the scene of a cardiac arrest." And then he continued with the instruction.

It went to show that no matter how disgusting a call got, it was an honor to save someone's life, just as Garry and Dennis had done for the patient with the colostomy. It stayed in the back of my head that if I could work through something as gruesome as that, I could still save someone's life.

I worked on many calls with Garry. Every time I was on a call with him, I felt it was an honor and a privilege to work with him. He kept everything simple and to the point.

One day I told him, "You are probably the best AEMT in the company."

"No way," he said, "I might be the best IV starter, but definitely not the best AMT."

He wasn't bragging about being a good IV starter. It was true. I had seen him start many IV lines, and he very rarely missed the vein.

Even though he insisted that he was not the best AMT, however, I still considered him one of the best.

I would learn more and hear other war stories the days I'd stop at the firehouse on my way home from school at New York Tech. I would stop if I saw someone there. Sometimes I would see Tom Koskey cleaning the truck or Paul Abbruzzese just hanging around. When I was new to the company, in particular, I found these guys very good to talk to and I learned a few simple things from listening to them.

One time I helped Tom with truck-clean-up detail. While I was stocking one of the cabinets, I saw a bottle of whiskey. I thought this was odd because most of the guys in the company were not heavy drinkers.

I said, "Hey Tom. What's with the bottle of booze?"

Tom said, "You'll find out someday."

I looked at the bottle. I knew it wasn't for pleasure. I figured maybe it was used as medicine or something.

Finally, Tom said, "If you do mouth-to-mouth and the patient pukes in your mouth, or if you see a real disgusting sight, it's the best thing to settle your stomach."

Tom was good at explaining how to deal with realistic situations. While I was playing with the equipment and learning how to use it, for example, he would explain how to brace yourself in a fast-moving truck while using the resuscitator.

Whenever I saw Paul Abbruzzese at the firehouse, he was usually sitting on a chair in front, and I would stop to talk to him. He told me a story once, which had happened in 1977. There was a house fire in which someone had used a flammable liquid to set himself on fire in the attic. Before water was put on the fire, Paul was doing a search and rescue. It was not known at that point that the case was an apparent suicide. Paul found the victim in the attic and dragged him out; the victim was pronounced dead at the scene.

As I was to find out, Paul, as did I and many others in the company, had found it difficult to prove himself in the beginning. As I mentioned previously, it was hard to prove yourself in the volunteer fire service. Sometimes, particularly in the daytimes when everyone was at work, it was easier to get hands-on experience. But at other times, when everyone was available to respond, you would often be up against a job that required only three or four people, when you had ten members who wanted to give a helping hand. This fire and suicide case was Paul's moment to prove his ability to do the job.

"Some people are easily accepted, while others have to work harder to prove themselves to the company," he told me. "You are the kind that has difficulty. I also had that problem. But God sometimes works in funny ways. You just have to wait for the opportunity. My opportunity came when the man set himself on fire and I went in and got him out.

"Kevin Tholl, who had the same problem," he told me, "cleared out a choking person's airway in Roy Rogers." He paused. "Sometimes, Dan, I think you are afraid of making a mistake. Don't be afraid to do something wrong, because nobody in this company is perfect."

Another time, during a drill in which we were simulating an accident, I was very confused about what to do. After the drill, Paul came up to me and said, "Dan, don't be afraid of making a mistake. Do something. Fake it if you have to. Don't worry about fucking up. If you fuck up, we will cover you. You've got to have more confidence in yourself."

A few weeks later, we had a cardiac arrest call, and for the first time, I did mouth-to-mouth. After the call was over, he said, "Dan, come here."

I walked with him into the company room alone.

"Nice work," he said.

"You think so?"

"You did something," Paul said. "You didn't stand around with your thumb up your ass. That's what I like to see."

Dad, I Broke the Side Door

When I was eighteen, I thought I was an adult and fully mature. Well, maybe physically, but that was about it. By the time I entered the fire department, I was twenty. I was completing my third year of college and thought I had my head on perfectly straight. Now that I am in my forties, I realize what it meant when people said that I still had a lot of growing up to do.

When I started out in the fire department, I made my work there my priority, at the expense of looking for real work. I treated it like it was my livelihood even though I was only a volunteer.

At the end of my junior year in college, my parents were away and I was home alone. I don't think I had classes on this particular day. The radio sounded a rescue call. It came over as a back injury. At this stage of my volunteer career as a fireman, I could not miss a call unless I was out of town or in school. So I jumped out of bed, put my pants on, and ran out of my house. The air horns were blowing a 22. That meant a rescue call. I reached into my pocket to find my car keys, only to find out that my pockets were empty—which meant that I had put on the wrong pair of pants. I felt that I had to do everything possible to make the rescue truck, so I ran to the side door of my house only to find it locked.

I thought, "Now what should I do?" I went to the garage, took a broom, and broke the glass on the side door. Then I ran upstairs, got the keys, and off I went to the call. There was no way I could have made the truck, so I drove straight to the location of the call.

Upon my arrival, I asked Chief Jim Fairben if they needed anything from the truck.

"No," he said, "but they may need you to help carry the patient down, because it is an obese woman and they can use whatever manpower they can get."

I walked further into the courtyard of the apartment complex and was told by someone else, "We got enough guys to carry her. Take this and put it back in the truck." He handed me the trauma kit.

I took the kit to the truck and by the time I turned around, they were already wheeling the patient onto the county bus for transport to Nassau Hospital.

Afterward, we were put on a Signal 13, which meant we were to return to our headquarters and homes.

On my drive back home, I said to myself, "How am I going to explain the broken window to my father?"

It would have been a comedy show if a cop had seen me trying to break into my own house, thinking I was a burglar. When I arrived home, I cleaned up the glass that had shattered all over the side stoop. Later on that night, my father called to see how things were going with me being home alone.

I said, "You're not going to like this."

"Oh no," he said. "Now what!"

"Well, I was called out on an emergency, and I went to my car and found that my car keys were in my other pants pocket—"

He interrupted. "You locked yourself out of the house and you had to break in."

"How did you guess? I broke the storm door window to get in."

He laughed. "Gee, you're a real clown."

I said, "I'm glad that you're not mad."

"No, I'm not mad because I don't have to pay to have it replaced. You do."

Well, I did pay to have the window replaced and, with that, squared everything with my dad. Now, when I think about it, I wonder why I didn't think about just missing one call and finding a more sensible way to get into my house.

Man Collapsed While Mowing His Lawn

It was May of 1979. A nice, sunny afternoon. Kids were out of school for the day and I was driving home from classes, when I heard the horns blow a 22. I raced to the firehouse to make the truck.

I heard someone say that a man had collapsed while mowing his lawn.

"This could be an arrest," I heard someone else say.

I went in the back of the rescue truck, set up the resuscitator, and prepared for the worst. The truck pulled away and raced to the scene with its siren blaring. While I was fixing the oxygen in preparation for a cardiac arrest, I saw Paul Szymanski stick his head up into the cab. He wanted to hear what the situation was from the man riding shotgun.

After a moment, he pulled his head back and said in a professional tone of voice, "Full arrest. Have that oxygen ready."

As we pulled up to the scene, I saw CPR being administered. Louie Mancuso was doing mouth-to-mouth. I didn't want to keep him waiting, so I rushed over with the resuscitator. Louie quickly put the mask over the patient's mouth and nose, and forced the oxygen into his lungs. John Bennett was attempting to start an IV. I remember the patient's wife standing nearby. She seemed more fascinated with what we were doing for her husband than upset about her husband being clinically dead and about to perish. Lieutenant John Bennett ordered the Reeves stretcher, and we packaged the dying patient on itReeves with CPR in progress.

When we were set to carry the patient out to the truck, Lieutenant Bennett said, "Okay, let's go with him." We had to interrupt CPR for about five seconds to carry him from his front lawn and to the rescue truck. Once he was on the bunk, we immediately resumed CPR. Paul Szymanski was on compressions and I took the resuscitator mask and placed it over the man's nose and mouth. The truck pulled away with the siren wailing.

Here, in the truck, was the first time I ever did CPR on a live person. Yes, I was a little nervous, but had to do the best I could. Szymanski was doing the one-thousand counts on the compressions, and Kevin McDermott, from Reliance Engine 2, had to show me how to place both my hands, with one holding the patient's chin and the mask to form an airtight seal, so the air would go into the patient's lungs. Of course, I was using my other hand to press the button in front of the mask, to force oxygen into the patient. When we arrived at Nassau Hospital, Kevin took over the ventilations, and I ran out to get a hospital stretcher from the ER.

As I was running to get it, I saw Captain Ostipwko step out of his van and yell, "Danny, walk!"

I slowed down to a brisk walk, grabbed the stretcher, and took it to the truck. They carried him out of the truck and placed him on the wheeled hospital stretcher and resumed CPR. A team of doctors and nurses was waiting for us outside the ER.

While I was wheeling him to the cardiac trauma room, I heard a nurse saying, "Witnesses say he collapsed while mowing his lawn, and this rescue squad brought him in."

They tried to get his heart going again in the trauma room to no avail. The patient was pronounced dead.

Later on that night, I was talking to Paul about the incident.

"How did that cardiac arrest make out?" I asked. I did not know he'd died, because he hadn't been pronounced dead until about a half an hour after we'd left the hospital.

Paul said, "He died."

"I used the resuscitator for the first time," I said.

Paul said, "That's good. That's the most important job in CPR, because you got to get that air in the lungs."

"I guess the compressions are just as important, because the ventilations are no good unless you get that blood and oxygen circulating."

"True," replied Paul.

I said, "It would have been nice if I'd saved him, since it was my first time doing CPR on a real person."

"Well, you can't save everyone," Paul said. "You are going to see a lot of people die in this company."

A Drill Come True

IT WAS OFTEN SAID THAT, as soon as we had a drill, we would get a call that would allow us to use the skills that were taught at that drill. For example, the AEMTs once had a drill on how to use a pair of military antishock trousers, also known as the MAST suit. If a patient has abnormally low blood pressure, you fit the trousers onto the patient's legs, and blow the MAST suit up like a balloon. This tightens the blood vessels in the patient's lower body and raises the blood pressure enough to get oxygen to the brain. Sure enough, right after that drill, we had a call that required us to use the MAST suit.

My first drill come true happened sometime after the weather started to get warmer in 1979. The drill was a lesson on the use of the portapower. The portapower, in those days, was akin to the Jaws of Life, a motorized tool now used to pry open a car door that can't be opened due to damage caused by an accident. We didn't have a motor-operated Jaws of Life tool back then; we had only the portapower, which was hand-operated. Whereas you only need one man to operate the motorized tool, with the manually operated tool, you need one man to pump—as if pumping a jack—and another man to place the jaw in a car door. Lieutenant John Bennett conducted the drill.

Sure enough, soon afterward, we were called to a car accident in which we were to use this tool. The accident was on Plainfield Avenue behind Floral Park Memorial High School. I remember riding in the truck on the way to the call and they were calling for the portapower tool. As we pulled up to the scene, there was a car wrapped around a telephone pole, with one person trapped in the backseat. It was apparent that he hadn't been wearing a seat belt. The force of the accident had sent him backward from the driver's seat through the space in between the front bucket seats, and then into the backseat. We were concerned that he may have sustained internal injuries.

Two men were assigned to operate the jaws. Another man and I were assigned to hose detail. My partner hooked up the hose to the fire hydrant, and I held the nozzle. Then we stood at the ready in case a fire started. If it did, we could put water on the fire without unnecessary delay. As I was standing by with the hose, I peered into the crowd of onlookers and saw Marc Krauss. His company had not been called to this case. Therefore, he was not required to participate in the rescue operation. In less than a half an hour, the door was pried open. We immobilized the patient and sent him to the hospital by county police ambulance.

It turned out that the man trapped in the car had only a couple of superficial bruises with no internal injuries. He was released from the hospital later that day.

I came home from school a few days later and found Marc Krauss talking to my father in the backyard. When Marc saw me, he turned and said, "You guys did a good job at that accident the other day. I was really impressed."

Soon after, we had another occasion to use this tool. Summer had set in. It couldn't have been more than two months after the accident in back of the high school. However, the person in second accident was not as lucky as the first victim.

I was on summer vacation, and was awakened at home at about 3:00 or 4:00 in the morning. The call was for an auto accident, with the car on fire being located near a house. Once the police dispatcher heard that it was near a house, he was required to dispatch all five companies to the scene. I quickly got dressed and ran across the street. We raced to the scene and, upon our arrival, we saw an overturned auto. I left Engine 3 and waited for Rescue to arrive. I saw Pete Van Tassel run to the alert truck to set up the hose line. I noticed he was moving more quickly than usual, so I knew this was something big. I overheard people saying that someone was trapped in the car.

The rescue truck pulled up seconds later, but the alert engine, as it had been the first engine on the scene, was assigned to handle the fire. I got inside the rescue truck and put on my turnout gear. When I stepped back out, Lieutenant Bennett was calling for the portapower.

As I approached the car, the fire was pretty much out, but there was smoke coming from the engine. I saw probationary firefighter Kevin Green handling the nozzle. He was being instructed by his company officers to put a low-pressure spray on the understructure of the overturned car. I looked inside the car and saw an unconscious man bleeding from the nose. I was assigned to pump the jack while Pete Walters tried to open the door with the jaws. Rescue Company firefighter Jim Friedman crawled into the car and administered an IV solution of lactated ringers after making sure that the patient's airway was clear. Lactated ringers is an IV solution used to replenish the patient's electrolytes.

The chief in charge called for the Nassau Police mini-rescue truck along with the police ambulance. Meanwhile, the police emergency services arrived. They were equipped with a motorized tool, also known as the Jaws of Life. The county cop walked over to the car with the jaws in his hand. He placed his jaws where the door opened. As the jaws opened up, the door literally fell off the vehicle. I guess our tool must have loosened the door enough for it to come off completely when the more superior tool was used. Nassau County Police Officer Sherman took charge of immobilizing the patient. He called for a cervical collar and a short spine board. He put the cervical collar and the backboard on the patient to immobilize his head and spine. Once this was done, we moved the patient onto the longboard stretcher, and from there, onto the wheeled trundle. Officer Sherman and some of our men traveled in the ambulance to the hospital.

The rest of us were put on a Signal 13. By the time we got to the firehouse, daylight was setting in. It was about 5:30 in the morning. I stayed to help put the equipment back on the truck and replace used supplies. We were allowed to go home after the truck was ready for service for the next call.

When I got home I wrote a note to my parents: "Don't wake me up. I was up since four in the morning at a car accident." Then I went straight to bed.

The patient remained in critical condition for a few days and subsequently expired in the hospital. I later learned that John Perry from Engine 1, the Alert Company, had called the fire in since it had happened right in front of his house. After calling, he had put his garden hose on the fire to get it under control before the trucks arrived.

The patient's father was among the spectators at the scene, but as the car had belonged to a friend of the patient's, and the father didn't know that it was his son who was critically injured and trapped in the car.

John Perry described meeting the young man's father later. He said, "The father came over my house when he heard that I was the one who made the call. He thanked me for calling and for putting the fire out."

Probie School

It is a requirement that all probationary firefighters attend fire school in Bethpage, Long Island. When I went in 1979, there were seven classes we had to take. We needed one class about ropes and knots, one class about masks, one about fire extinguishers, two classes about ladders, and two about hoses. Since I was a probationary firefighter at that time, I was required to take all of these classes. Classes started in the late spring and ran for seven consecutive Fridays, and I would be taking them with two other guys from the company.

On my first night of probie training, Lieutenant Paul Abbruzzese called to remind me that school was starting that night. The three of us were to meet at the main firehouse and go together. At the firehouse, I saw Paul.

"Okay Dan," he said. "Get your gear ready." I got my gear off of the rescue truck and went to the floodlight truck, which would be taking us to fire school. There was the driver, Kevin Green, and I. Kevin and I sat in the back of the truck for the ride.

Kevin was a quiet, wide-eyed, nice kid when he first started in the fire department. He impressed me as the kind of new boy on the block that did whatever you told him to do. At every routine fire call, he would follow orders the way he had at that accident with the overturned auto. In other words, he respected his officers and the seniority of other members. Little did we think back then that Kevin would become fourth assistant chief in April of 1989 and work his way up to chief of the department in April of 1993.

The first night of fire school I learned rope and knots. The most commonly used knots were the clove hitch and the bowline. These were the two knots that I put into use when I took the Basic Rescue course later.

A chief from the East Meadow Fire Department taught us about masks, or self-contained breathing apparatuses. He taught us how to turn the mask on and how to bleed out when turning it off. He showed us how to take care of the masks and the accompanying air bottles that rest on our backs. After this instruction, he took us to the smoke house. There, we all had to put our masks on. Before sending us into the smoke house, he did an inspection to make sure that everyone had his or her gear on properly.

My mask was fogging up when I saw his silhouette standing in front of me.

He asked me, "How long have you been in the fire department?"

"Since January, Chief," I answered.

"What's wrong with those boots?" he asked. I looked down and saw that my boots were folded down and not pulled up. I then pulled up my boots, and the chief went on with his inspection.

Next, we were all assigned partners. The chief yelled out to us, "Remember your partner. You are responsible for him, and he is responsible for you."

Then it was time for us to enter the smoke house. We had to enter the building on one side and exit from the other side. At first, I was a little nervous. However, once in the smoke house, I was enjoying every minute of it. I could not see a thing. It was like going through a maze trying to find your way to the exit. All I could hear were the other firefighters yelling through their masks, and I remembered what the chief had said about our being responsible for one another. So I just followed the man in front of me by touching his boot and helping the man behind me until we all found our way out of the smoke house.

The class on fire extinguishers was taught by a chief from the Jericho Fire Department. This instructor knew how to make us laugh, but he also had a serious streak to him. He would say to us, "Nobody likes to fuck around more than I do, but you have to realize the hazards you are up against in the fire service." He taught how to attack a fire with a spray stream rather than a straight stream. He started a fire and then we, the newcomers, had to put the fire out with an extinguisher, while he'd stand back and say things like, "Come on, get in there and fight that fire."

One probationary firefighter from another department was trying to attack the fire with a water extinguisher when the hose of the extinguisher fell off. He looked at the instructor for instruction. The instructor said, "What do you do if your dick falls off? You don't look at me. You pick it up and put it back on." I guess we all learned from that. The kid picked up the hose, put it back on the extinguisher, and continued putting the fire out.

We also learned about the CO2 extinguisher, which is used on electrical and grease fires. The chief instructor demonstrated how the extinguisher worked, pulling the pin out of the lock mechanism and discharging the chemicals over a large area.

As mentioned, we needed two classes about hose operation. The chief instructor of both was a member of the Oyster Bay Atlantic Steamer Fire Department. We gathered outside the building and listened to him lecture.

One of the things he said was, "When you pull up to a fire scene, you want to do as professional a job as possible. People don't want to hear any of your shit about how you are just a volunteer. They call you to help them, so you help them…. Now we're going to teach you how to get rid of your fear of going in a fire."

We gathered inside the building and the chief instructor set a bundle of wood in the middle of the floor on fire.

"If any one of you doesn't feel good," he said, "none of this macho shit. We don't want you getting sick, so if you have to leave, I'll understand." Then he said, "Take off your gloves and feel above your heads." The heat of the fire was getting closer and closer to the floor.

We exited the building and set the hoses up and practiced attacking the fire. We had such a good time that we continued the process, starting about five or six fires and putting each one out. That way, everyone had a chance to get some hands-on experience.

For this class, Marc Krauss had come along for the ride and participated. He had already passed probationary fire school, but sometimes members go back to probationary classes just to keep their skills up to date.

Marc had told me, "This is the way you get the feel of a fire and swallow your fears."

We also had two classes about ladders. They showed us how to raise a ladder with two people. One person knelt on the bottom rung while the other raised the ladder. That was to prevent the ladder from sliding while it was being raised. We learned other safety measures, as well, such as using care not to disrupt electrical wires that may be in the way. We practiced climbing up and down the ladders to overcome any fear of heights. We also learned how to do a leg lock. When a fireman was working on a ladder, he may be stationary on top of the ladder, either opening a window, passing equipment through a window, or what have you. By doing a leg lock in such a position—that is, by putting one leg through the rung and locking your foot on the lower rung—you wouldn't fall if you lost your balance.

I was fascinated by fire school. It was the foundation of my firefighting skills and experience, even though my main job was still in emergency medical services. I had entered the fire department to help sick and injured people; however, when I became friendly with Marc Krauss, an engine man, I became more enchanted with the firefighting aspects of the job.

Four Back-to-Back Calls in June 1979

The first Wednesday in June started out like any normal day. I was keeping a mental note that we were to have our company meeting that night and made sure I didn't make any social plans.

Early in the afternoon, I paid Marc Krauss a visit at his house. We were in his backyard talking when we overheard the sirens going off. It was a 22—a rescue call. I had to go.

Before I even said anything, Marc said, "Bye, Dan."

I ran to my car and planned to head to the firehouse, when a police car passed by and made a turn down the next street. I followed him. I pulled up to the scene with the cop and saw ex-Chief Bobby Meehan pull up in his car. We went into the house together, and right in the foyer was a bed with an eighty-four-year-old man screaming from abdominal pain. Bobby took his pulse and respiration rate. We waited for the truck to respond. The Nassau Police ambulance was also on the way. Every second that passed seemed like a minute, and every minute an hour.

Finally, the truck pulled up. A second call came over for a possible stroke, the location of which was only a few blocks away. So we kept the stair chair and a trauma kit at the scene of the first call, while the truck left and went to the second call. Captain Mike Ostipwko was in charge of the second call, and Bobby Meehan went with him. Left back at the first call were Ed Fry, Noel Beebe, and me. There was not much more that we could do for a man with abdominal pain except wait for the ambulance to arrive. The man's wife was giving us her husband's medical history. She told us that he was diabetic and had a heart condition. As the ambulance pulled up, she moved the end table next to the bed, saying, "I'll get this out of your way."

I felt relief that the ambulance had arrived because this man was in a lot of pain. We decided to carry him out on the stair chair and transfer him to the trundle in front of the house. I was told to get the trundle and place it in the pathway leading to the front door. I went out to the bus and asked Kevin Green to assist me. He willingly helped. While we were moving the trundle, others were carrying the man out of the house.

His wife was going to go with him in the ambulance. She had a coat on, even though it was late spring, with summer just around the corner; everyone else was wearing tank tops or short-sleeved shirts. She was outside with us, but then said that she had to go back into the house for something. Meanwhile, we were transferring the husband onto the trundle. As I was buckling the seat belt to strap him on, I heard a loud scream, as though someone were being murdered. It was a horrible sound. I knew it was the man's wife. Having once heard a woman scream like that from back pain, for a split second, I thought that she had pulled her back out.

Sergeant Macintosh of the Floral Park Police radioed in a third rescue call at the same address as the first. I went in the house and saw Ed Fry holding the woman in his arms. He told me to get the stair chair, so I went and got the same chair we had just used to carry her husband out. Her husband was now sitting straight up on the trundle on the front lawn. I went back in the house and saw the man's wife lain out on the floor, with Ed Fry administering CPR on her.

"No, this can't be," I thought.

Ed called for the ambu-bag and an oral airway. I quickly gave him both. The woman was now making a rattling noise as she breathed, something called agonal respirations. I felt for a radial pulse and found none. Noel Beebe checked for a carotid pulse and found none. Pete Walters, who worked a few blocks away, entered the room and started CPR compressions, while Ed Fry was administering ventilations using the ambu-bag. Once Pete started in on the compressions, the patient began vomiting profusely. The vomit poured all over Ed's lap. We heard the siren of the rescue truck responding once again, back from the scene of the second call that had just happened.

"Danny, go to the truck and get the suction unit," Noel said.

I ran out just as the truck was pulling up, hurried to the back of the truck, and grabbed the suction unit. Back in the house, the vomiting still hadn't stopped; every CPR compression only resulted in the patient vomiting more, and now the vomit was all over both Ed and Noel. As Noel began suctioning, I started wondering whether the Rescue Company was really for me.

The Nassau ambulance assigned to handle the stroke was now also responding to this scene. So Mike Ostipwko decided to take the stroke victim and the man with abdominal pain to the hospital in the rescue truck, and to use the ambulance to transport the woman.

A Nassau cop from the ambulance came in and tapped me on the shoulder. "Are you family?"

"No," I replied. "I'm from Rescue in the fire department."

So the cop gave me the IV bag, as Jim Friedman attempted to put the IV on the woman.

Once the Nassau cop had the telemetry hooked up, he said into his radio, "Cardiac Base, this is 2-3-6-3 on the air with a run. Cardiac arrest." He attempted to get ahold of the base several times.

Meanwhile, with CPR still in progress, we put the woman on a Reeves stretcher and carried her out. We put her on the trundle, wheeled her to the ambulance, and loaded her inside. The Nassau cop, the Nassau AEMT originally assigned to the stroke victim, Ed Fry, and Jim Friedman were to ride in the back of the ambulance with her. Jim Friedman was doing the compressions at this point, while Ed Fry continued doing ventilations with the resuscitator.

Ed moved back away from the patient, interrupting CPR for a few seconds, as soon as he heard someone say, "Clear." The Nassau AEMT charged the defibrillator and shocked her once. The patient turned blue. Once CPR was resumed, however, the patient's color became less cyanotic.

Then with Officer Ken Rowlands of the Floral Park Police at the wheel, they took off and transported her to Nassau Hospital.

The rest of us went back into the house to clean up the mess we'd left behind. There were needles, gauze pads, and other things of the sort. Noel wiped the vomit off the floor, and then walked into the kitchen. I needed a drink of water, so I followed him.

He turned and looked at me. "You okay, Danny?"

"Yes, I'm hanging in there," I replied. "I just need a drink of water."

Noel got himself a glass of water as well, rinsed out his mouth, and spit in the sink. The water he spit out had a tint of the vomit that had come from the patient.

"When someone chucks in your mouth," he said, "that should wet your whistle."

He must have tried mouth-to-mouth when I'd been out retrieving the suction unit. He cleaned the vomit off his pants and shirt.

After we were done cleaning up, I drove him back to the firehouse. I decided to hang out until Ed and Jim returned, to find out how the woman had made out. I saw Noel and Chief Rickie Maickels by the bathroom. The chief was holding the suction unit. Its container was still filled with the vomit that had been suctioned out of the woman's throat.

Figuring I could get out of this one, I started to walk downstairs, when the chief said, "Get over here, Danny. Don't be bashful."

I walked back over to them. "How do you clean that thing out?"

"I'm going to show you." He twisted off the container and handed it to me.

I took it and poured it down the slop sink.

Noel said, "Just turn your head and don't look at it."

I turned my head away, and just kept taking deep breaths and swallowing. This part was actually not so bad. I had cleaned up vomit before. I was just still in a state of shock over seeing a woman alive and well one minute, and in cardiac arrest the next.

Finally, the Nassau Police ambulance pulled up to drop off Ed and Jim.

Jim was carrying some of our equipment into the firehouse, when I approached him. "How did she make out?" I asked.

He said in a low voice, "She died."

Just when I was ready to go home, we received another rescue call. This time it was a child in convulsions.

As we were pulling up to the scene in the rescue truck, Bob Lozraites was carrying the girl out to meet us. He later described her as having a fever high enough that his arms felt like they had been burning. At that time, we did not have any medications to use to bring her fever down, so we took the child to a Doctor Buckley's office for a shot. Afterward, we took her to the hospital.

Back at the firehouse, with the way the day was going, some of us stayed for a while, in case we had another call. I was one of them. It wasn't until around dinnertime that I finally got home. As I pulled into the driveway, I could not wait to vent about what happened that day.

I walked in the side door. My mother was fixing dinner. "I heard a lot of emergency signals go off," she said. "One was on Oak Street, and then Cherry Street—and then it sounded like they were called back to the same address on Oak Street."

I felt kind of sick now, thinking about seeing that lady go into cardiac arrest. I was reminded of my own mortality. I said, "We had an abdominal pain on Oak Street, then a stroke on Cherry Street, and then the man with the abdominal pain well, his wife dropped dead right in front of me."

My mother called into the other room. "Frank, did you hear that?"

My dad walked into the dining room with us, ready to hear what had happened.

My mother repeated to him what I had told her, as we sat down to eat our dinner. I can remember having London broil. While we were eating, my mother kept asking questions about it.

"Please," I said, "I can't talk about it." I normally liked to tell disgusting war stories at the dinner table. Before, I had always thought I was being funny. Well, what goes around comes around. This time, I was not in the mood.

"Well, now you know how *we* feel when you talk about these things at the dinner table," she said.

Later on, I went back to the firehouse for our monthly meeting. While there, I stopped to talk to Paul Abbruzzese.

"That fucked me up when that lady died today," I said.

"Yes, it can be a little upsetting," Paul said. Ed Rothenberg told me that I would see worse.

At the end of the meeting, we had hot dogs. I saw Ed Fry talking about the call to someone. I approached him and said, "You did nice work on that lady today."

"So did you," he told me. "You did all right."

Yes, I had stayed with the patient, but I felt that I could have handled myself a little better emotionally.

Later that night, I talked some more about it with my mother.

"That's so sad," she said. "Who's going to take care of the husband?"

The next day, I also mentioned the incident to one of my neighbors, Mrs. McCabe, and she told me that she had seen her mother die in the same manner.

She said, "Dying can be as fast as blowing out a lit match."

Take a Deep Breath and Pitch In

One night after a call, Ed Fry was driving me back to the firehouse, when he asked, "Anybody giving you a hard time?"

"Sometimes," I replied.

"That goes away in time. You're doing a good job.... Does the sight of blood bother you?"

"No, blood doesn't bother me too much," I said. "It's when someone pukes that makes me cringe."

"Well, they say when you are confronted with a messy situation, you just take a deep breath and pitch in."

Another time, I complimented him again on the job he had done on the woman who'd died in front of us.

"Oh boy, that was a mess," he said.

"It sure was. I got pretty upset over that call."

With a cigar sticking out of his mouth, and towering over me with his six-foot frame, Ed laughed and said, "Oh, for Chrissake. I saw a woman dead in the bathtub with both of her wrists slashed."

Another case that I thought Ed did a good, professional job on was one where the patient was apparently strung out on angel dust. I was awakened at about two or three in the morning by loud talking. It was summertime, and my bedroom window was open. I looked out the window and saw two teenage kids walking by fast. I could not hear too much of what they were saying. All I knew was that they seemed stressed out and out of breath. Someone was apparently chasing them.

My first guess was that the police were chasing them, because I saw a cop suspiciously patrolling the street only seconds later. I knew one of the guys from the neighborhood. He was notorious for using angel dust in those days.

I ignored the situation because the police were obviously already onto them, and tried to go back to sleep. Just before I dosed off, I was awaken by the radio signal for a rescue call. It came over as an arm laceration at police headquarters. I rushed to get dressed, and ran downstairs and out to my car. All the while, I had a gut feeling that this call would be related to one of those two clowns who'd passed in front of my house.

Jim Friedman and I both pulled up to the police station in our private cars, and walked in together. Sure enough, it was one of the kids I'd seen, but there was also blood all over the squad room. I observed what appeared to be an avulsion on his arm. He had a cut radial artery and was squirting blood all over the squad room, while yelling and screaming.

He was shouting obscenities at Police Officer John Donnely. "Donnely, you mother fucker, you suck my dick!"

Officer Ried approached Jim and me. "We're trying to calm him down. See if you can approach him, but, if he resists and acts violent, the hell with it." Ried was concerned about our safety first.

As Jim and I walked toward the squad room, the patient screamed, "Get the fuck out of here. You're not sticking any needles in me!"

Ried called us back. He apparently didn't want anything to happen to Jim or me. The patient pulled the drawers out of the desk he was handcuffed to and flung them across the room. Then he took Ried's hat, spit on it, and flung it at Donnely.

"That's mine!" Ried told him.

"Sorry," the patient said, "You're all right. But Donnely is a scumbag."

When Chief Rickie Maickels arrived on the scene, he ordered Jim and me to go outside since there was not much we could do at that time.

I remember walking down the steps and hearing Jim say, "Holy shit."

I looked where he was looking and saw that the window to the squad room where the patient was had been broken, and had blood all over it. It looked like someone had taken a can of red paint and splashed it all over the window.

From the window, we heard, "Donnely! You suck. Donnely! Your mother wears army boots."

It was going to take a miracle to calm this guy down.

Ed Fry had arrived at this point. The patient's father and older brother arrived shortly thereafter, and tried to calm the patient down. Chief Maickels had specifically called Fry into the police station, since Fry did have a nice way about him in these kinds of situations. I forget who else went inside, but I think Paul Abbruzzese and Terry Carney were there. The rest of us stayed outside, since too many people would only aggravate the situation.

Finally, the yelling and screaming stopped. I looked up at the blood-splattered window and saw Ed Fry smiling and talking to the patient, while others were dressing his wounds. The patient had finally calmed down.

Currently, we did not have a permanent ambulance. Over the summer of 1979, however, we rented out an ambulance to use in lieu of the county police ambulance. But in this case, because we were dealing with an irrational individual under the influence of a controlled substance, we called the county police ambulance to transport him. We requested they transport the patient to the Nassau County Medical Center in East Meadow, since it had a psychiatric emergency unit.

When the county ambulance pulled into the driveway, Chief Rickie Maickels approached the AMT. "We have a patient on angel dust. He is very violent, so be careful what you say and do." They both went into the stationhouse.

Paul Abbruzzese then came out and said, "Wait till you see this. We have him facedown and handcuffed behind his back."

A few minutes passed and they carried the patient out in the position that Paul had described, with the boy's father following closely behind.

"Dad, go home and go to bed," the patient said.

"No," his father replied. "I'll meet you at the hospital."

As his father walked away from the ambulance and toward his car, he humbly said to us, "Thank you very much, fellows. I'm sorry this had to be."

After the ambulance left, Garry Gronert and I went back into the squad room to retrieve our equipment. The whole room was splattered with blood. It turned out that after the patient was arrested, he had become violent and tried to jump out the closed window.

As Garry and I were looking around for our equipment, he said, "Only one time I saw more blood than this. It was when the guy stabbed himself in the throat."

Back at the station, we went down to our company room and had coffee and pastries—a tradition after early-morning calls.

That was a tough summer for me. I faced a lot of discouragement. However, it was also a good summer because it taught me quite a bit. For instance, one time we had a call at Floral Park Memorial High School. It came over as "man collapsed while jogging." Sure enough, when we pulled up, we saw Chief Jim Fairben doing CPR on the patient.

I grabbed the suction and someone screamed at me, "Put that back!" He then grabbed it out of my hand and threw it on the bench in the ambulance. Tom Koskey later told me that I should only grab the suction if someone calls for it.

All I ended up doing on that call was to assist in putting the patient on the trundle. Others put him in the ambulance and then Chief Fairben gave me his keys and told me to drive the chief's car back to the firehouse. At that point, the ambulance disappeared, making its way to the hospital.

Later on that day, I pulled my car up next to a police car, and asked Officer Paul Weterau how the guy made out.

"Dead," he said, without emotion. "Twenty-two years old."

Police Officer Richie Meyers had had to tell the young man's father what had happened to his son.

A few years later, I was on a call with Meyers, when he again had to tell a family member that his loved one was dead.

"I hate that shit," Meyers said. "With the kid that died on the Memorial track, I went to his house and told his father that his son was rushed to the hospital. He asked me if his son is all right. I said, 'I'm afraid he passed away.' Then his father collapsed."

Thank God I never had to break that kind of news to anyone. That was usually the job of the police.

Sometime that summer, we had two drills at the Floral Park Memorial High School. Both were a disaster for me. I did not do well at all. The first drill was doing a rope slide down the side of the building. Everyone did it. When it was my turn, I put on the belt and whoever connected the rope to it abruptly pushed me off the roof, inadvertently knocking the wind out of me. I could not breathe, and Ed Fry was holding the rope, so I could not move.

I finally caught my breath enough to yell, "Let go!" and then slowly slid down, trying to recover the rest of my breath.

Then Paul Funk and Hugo Berta had to be funny, so they climbed up the wall with no rope belt and no gloves, which were usually worn to prevent rope burns.

I must have looked concerned about it, because Ed Fry said, "Don't worry, Danny. I only caused one man to fall off the roof, and that was twenty-two years ago."

The next month's drill was a simulation of a car accident, with multiple patients. While doing the simulation, I was waiting to be told what to do, which was wrong, as you are supposed to look around to find something that has to be done.

Paul Abbruzzese yelled out at me, "Come on, Danny. You're an EMT. You should know what you're doing!"

At the end of the drill, we went back to the firehouse to put the equipment away, and then I went down to the company room. Paul found me and called me outside.

"Danny, you are a slow-paced person," he said. "There is nothing wrong with being slow. However, you have to learn to think fast. You are an intelligent person. Many of these guys are not intelligent, but they know the job and are quick thinkers. Intelligence and speed don't go hand in glove. You've got to have more confidence in yourself. You are too afraid of making a mistake. Believe me, nobody in this company is perfect. If you fuck up, we will cover for you. But, I don't think you will fuck up. You just have to do something."

"Now people are going to yell and scream at you. I'm sorry if I did tonight. After your probation is over, you can tell people to go to hell if they bust your balls. But for now, just remember you have to do something. If you don't have confidence in yourself, then the guys are not going to have confidence in you."

Not too long after that drill, we had a call for an overdose. I sped to the scene in my own car, and as I stopped at a stop sign, I saw Ed Rothenberg turning from the opposite direction. It was a good feeling because he was an AEMT at the time and this particular call called for an AEMT. At the scene, we pulled to the side of the road together and got out of our cars.

One of the cops was yelling "Cardiac arrest!"

Ed and I ran to the van where the victim was. Inside was Jim Friedman doing the CPR compressions and Pete Feehan doing mouth-to-mouth. In the back of my mind were Paul's words to me about doing something, even if it was just a little.

"Jim," I said. "Let me know when you get tired and I'll take over."

"Okay, Dan," he replied. He stayed on the compressions and was holding up pretty well.

In a matter of minutes the trundle was by the back of the van. We had a short distance from where the patient was to the trundle, so they quickly paused the CPR and we placed him on the trundle. The resuscitator was not close by, but I was—I was right by the patient's head. So as someone next to me resumed compressions, for the first time, I put my mouth to the patient's and blew one breath of air for every five CPR compressions.

Some civilian was holding our resuscitator and saying, "Come on, guys." It was apparently one of the patient's friends.

One of our guys took the resuscitator from the civilian and began using it to ventilate the patient. Then the patient was rushed to the hospital. Ed Rothenberg and I stayed back in town.

Back at the firehouse, I heard Ed Rothenberg say, "I thought Pete Feehan was going to get initiated really well. It sounded just like the guy was going to vomit right in Pete's mouth."

Then Paul Abbruzzese, the second lieutenant, said, "Dan, come here."

I followed him downstairs, wondering if I did something wrong. When we got to the company room, he shut the door behind us. I was thinking, "What did I do now?"

"Nice work," he said.

"You really think so?" I said.

"Well, you did something. You didn't stand around with your thumb up your ass. That's what I like to see."

The end result of the call was the patient being pronounced dead at the hospital from an apparent overdose.

The following Sunday, I was in church. During the Prayer of the Faithful, the speaker asked us to pray for the deceased and mentioned this patient's name. A well-dressed girl sitting next to me seemed shocked when they mentioned his name. She started to cry softly.

Sometimes, we refer to drug addicts as dirt bags. I guess we are all guilty of that, me included. The bottom line, though: he was still a human being. The same as the guy on angel dust in the police station. Therefore, when it came to helping these people, it was our job to give it our best shot—since we were in the business of saving lives.

Another memorable time that summer was the Basic Rescue course we took at Bethpage Fire Academy. I had to get certification in the course within three years of coming into the company, so I figured the best time to get it done was now, and get it over with. Chief Jim Bugler of the Baldwin Fire Department taught us. He was the best instructor I ever had at Bethpage Academy. I could not help learning from him. He would lecture and then ask for a volunteer, and I always stepped right up.

Chief Bugler was sort of a morale chief. He'd say, "If you drop the victim off the roof, then it's everybody's fault—not the officer's, not the person tying the knots—it's everybody's fault. Don't try to get yourself off the hook, because you weren't paying attention to the mistake being made that caused the accident to begin with."

He would have us demonstrate roof rescues, lowering a victim from the roof down to the ground. Another rescue operation we had to do was to extend a ladder from one roof to another of the same height. I volunteered to drag Pete Feehan, as the victim, across the ladder to the other roof. Another ladder rescue was done by placing the ladder from the ground up to the roof. On this demonstration, I was again the rescuer. I had to climb up the ladder. Then two other rescuers put Jim Friedman on the ladder with his legs straddled around it. I was to step down the ladder, lowering Jim to the ground. Jim teased me the whole way down, praying out loud for mercy.

After that, one of our guys was afraid of heights and refused to play the victim, saying, "I don't trust Danny."

The next day, though, I ran into Paul Abbruzzese, who said, "Good job at fire school, Dan." It sure felt good to get a compliment after having two bad drills earlier that summer.

With the fire department, you only get one chance to make a good first impression. If you don't, you have to work twice as hard to make a good second or third impression. That is what my fellow probie, Pete Feehan, and I had to do. But toward the end of the summer, my confidence started to build. I started to touch patients more. I took a pulse here and blood pressure there. I started to get good at what I did.

Like one time, we had an elderly woman who fell down a few steps and hurt her shoulder. I asked whether she remembered falling. She did, in fact, remember, so it was unlikely that she'd lost consciousness before falling. I took her pulse and checked her neurological functions. She had equal strength on both sides of her body. She was able to move her legs. It was therefore unlikely that she was having a stroke.

Paul Abbruzzese came in and I explained what was going on. He sat her up, since it was only her shoulder that was bothering her. Paul put a sling and a swathe on the injured shoulder. Then we placed her on the trundle and carried her out to the ambulance. It was a hot day and the air-conditioning was cranked up in the ambulance.

The lady said, "Gee, that feels good. I wish I could stay in here!" It was a good sign that she still had a sense of humor.

Pete was also gaining experience. For example, there was the time we were on our way to a call for a man who'd passed out getting into his car. Several of us were riding in the back of the ambulance, when Mike Ostipwko looked back from the captain's seat and yelled, "Full arrest!"

At the scene, they quickly put him on the stretcher and placed him in the ambulance. Pete had stayed in the ambulance and resumed the CPR compressions. I jumped in and was ready to go, but was told to stay back. Although it was disappointing, it did make sense, because it would be too risky to have two probies, Pete and I, working a cardiac arrest at once. If I remember correctly, that was Pete's first time doing CPR.

A day or two after this incident, I heard conflicting stories about the outcome. First, I heard the patient was revived, but was a vegetable. Then someone said that he was in intensive care, sitting up and talking to people. We didn't hear any news about the man passing away, however, and in most cases of cardiac arrest, no news is good news. The only time the police would get an update on the person's condition is when the patient expired. Therefore, this case counted as a save.

Not too long after that call, we had a call at Koenig's Restaurant. We pulled up to the front of the establishment, and a cop came up to us and said that there was a man in cardiac arrest. We went upstairs to the room where the patient was. There was a wedding reception going on. The band was still playing music, but nobody was dancing. On the floor was a man down, and CPR was in progress. On the middle of the floor were the bride and groom sitting on chairs. The bride obviously was in distress, almost like she was praying. The groom was holding his new wife's hand trying to console her. We eventually learned that the patient was the father of the bride. We carried her father down the stairs and into the ambulance.

The next day, at our department picnic in Eisenhower Park, I asked Chief Jim Fairben how the father of the bride made out.

He pointed his thumb down. "Down the tubes. He never made it."

As I heard one person later put it, instead of going on a honeymoon, they'd be going to a funeral.

At the picnic, they issued spring and fall jackets, which were kind of like windbreakers. It was September and the weather was starting to get cool. This was my first company jacket—red with a yellow Maltese cross. It made me feel a little more professional, as it marked me as a firefighter from Rescue. Before this point, I had only worn plain clothes that gave no indication that I was from the fire department. Little did I know that I was going to wear this jacket and experience just the thing that every newcomer to Rescue just couldn't wait to experience.

In a matter of days, I was hanging out at the firehouse, wearing my new jacket, feeling like a full-fledged Rescue man, when a call came over. The horns were sounding, but I could not make out the nature of the call.

Chief Billerdello was getting in his car, so I asked him, "What is it, Chief?"

"On Jericho Turnpike in front of the Merry Peddler. A man having a heart attack," he said, and with that, he got in his car and drove off to the scene.

Ex-Chief Ron Nahas arrived at the firehouse and got in the driver's seat of the ambulance. I rode shotgun. Ed Rothenberg ran toward the bus, while we were waiting for a crew. I opened the door to get out and let Ed sit in the front, since he was a senior member.

"Stay there," he said, and then ran around and jumped in the back. Then off we went.

As we pulled up to the scene, I saw Chief Jim Fairben and his brother Kenny doing CPR on the patient. Then I knew we had work to do. The patient was a big man of about six feet tall. I took in the Reeves stretcher and opened it up. Meanwhile, a Nassau County Police AMT named Timothy Jaccard inserted an esophageal gastric tube airway (EGTA) into the patient. We placed the patient on the Reeves and then on the trundle. We decided to use the Nassau Police ambulance instead of our own, since Tim Jaccard had started working on the patient.

While they were wheeling him over to the ambulance, Ed Rothenberg said, "Danny, jump in the ambulance, and get on the compressions when we wheel him in."

In those days, they were experimenting with putting the patient's head toward the back of the ambulance in cardiac arrest situations. In all other cases, the head went toward the front and the feet to the back. While I was standing in the back, they wheeled him in. I had to get this right since it was my very first time doing compressions. I quickly located the landmark and began massaging the patient's chest. Chief Jim Fairben was standing outside the back of the ambulance, doing ventilations with the resuscitator. Every fifth compression that I did, he would pump air into the patient's lungs. I looked at the chief while I was doing the compressions and saw him wink at me. This gave me the reassurance that I was doing all right. The chief then passed the ventilations onto Ed Rothenberg and shut the back doors.

Inside, Terry Carney and Tim Jaccard were working on administering advanced life support. Police Officer Robert Gallo pulled away at a comfortable speed; it felt like we weren't even moving. This was good, because you could do more effective CPR in a smooth-riding ambulance.

After doing compressions for a while, while Ed did the ventilations, Ed said, "Okay, Danny, let's switch."

So I got on ventilations and Ed resumed with compressions. We were about halfway to the hospital. Tim and Terry asked the driver to pull over, as they had received an order from Medical Control to defibrillate. Terry had been on the phone to medical control while Tim was operating the defibrillator. Ed and I were required to continue with the CPR until the AMT ordered us to stop, so he could shock the patient.

"Clear," Tim said.

I moved back, but Ed pushed me as far away from the patient as he possibly could. "Get the hell out of here," he said, meaning to get away from the patient and the trundle while the patient was being defibrillated.

"Okay," Tim said, "defibrillating on three. One-two-three.... " Then he shocked the patient.

The patient jolted and expelled gas from his mouth. There was no vomit since his esophagus was blocked off by the EGTA.

Ed said, "Okay, Danny, check for a carotid pulse."

I checked. "No pulse," I reported.

Ed and I resumed CPR. A little later, we got another order from Medical Control to defibrillate, and repeated the process. The same thing—no pulse. I looked out the window of the ambulance and saw that we were just around the corner from the hospital. We pulled up to the emergency room entrance, where the hospital staff had a crash team waiting for us. CPR was still in progress. The patient was pulled out of the ambulance and wheeled into the cardiac emergency treatment room. Tim Jaccard stayed in the treatment room while Ed, Terry, Officer Gallo, and I stayed outside.

As we waited, Officer Gallo told me what had happened before we arrived. "I pulled up to the scene. The wife told me that they'd just come from Roosevelt Field when the husband started having chest pains. When I saw him, he was unconscious. There was a faint pulse and shallow respiration. After the Fairbens arrived, he went into cardiac arrest and then they started CPR. I tried to keep the wife calm and take down the information."

Right then, I saw Tim Jaccard walk out of the cardiac treatment room. He walked toward us and gave two thumbs up.

I said, "You mean we brought him back?"

"Yes, we did!" he replied.

The patient's wife arrived in the emergency room just then, and Tim explained to her what was happening. "His heart is working again, but he is still in critical condition." He then showed her to the reception desk, so she could give the staff her husband's information.

On the way back to the firehouse, I asked, "How did I do, Ed?"

He said, "You did your job well, Dan. When I asked to change positions on the CPR, it didn't mean you were doing it wrong. After doing CPR for a long period of time, you get tired. Then the CPR is not as effective. So, we have to switch every now and then. You also did a good job on the ventilations."

Once we reached the firehouse, I had to go to the police station for the gas key, so we could gas up the ambulance. There, I saw Ken Fairben, and told him the good news about the man. I also asked him how I did, and he said he thought I did fine.

Gallo was behind the desk writing reports, and chimed in too. "You did good, Danny. I looked back and thought, 'Oh no, you're going to fuck up, you're going to fuck up!' But no, you did all right."

Fall Semester of 1979

THAT SUMMER, I ENROLLED IN a police officer civil service test-preparation class for the Suffolk County Police Department. This was, and still is, the highest paid police department in the nation. There was a lot of competition and very few vacancies for all of the candidates. I took the course during the summer and signed up to repeat it again toward the end of the summer. The test was divided into three categories. First, were judgment questions, then questions pertaining to how you would present written material, and finally reading comprehension questions.

I took the New York City Police test in June. That test was easy. If you knew how to spell your name right, you could score in the high nineties. However, the Suffolk test was harder. The judgment questions were based on situations that police officers encounter in their jobs. You had to use common sense in answering them. The second section of questions pertaining to preparing written material asked you to pick the answer that had several sentences in the correct order. The reading comprehension questions were based on reading passages. This test was a lot more ambiguous than the New York City Police test. I felt that you almost had to be a genius to score high on it. I knew that I could pass but could not score high enough to be appointed.

Toward the end of the summer, my parents and I went to Riverhead in Long Island to visit my aunt and uncle. Their neighbor was nice enough to let us stay in their house. Another neighbor named Phil was a friend of mine from when we were kids. He was planning to take the Suffolk Police test in November like I was. One night when I was there, we went out and did some carousing. We stopped at a tavern and had a few beers with his friends. Then we visited the home of another of his friends, who was a professor at Stony Brook University. It was a very nice home with a large living room. After we left there, Phil and I went home. The whole time, we were talking about the police test in November. He said he thought it would be an exciting job since he liked to drive fast.

Back home in Floral Park, I continued with the police-test course, taught by an inspector of the Nassau County Police Department. Another of the class instructors was a lieutenant in the New York City Police Department, and also taught at New York Tech in Manhattan, where I attended college.

September arrived and my college classes started. I took one class in life science, one political science class, and a few police science classes. The life science class was up my alley because it entailed a lot about the human body, which overlapped with my EMT training. The political science class was called "Basic Legal Concepts of the Administration of Justice," and had more to do with civil law than criminal law.

On my first day back, I walked into the classroom and recognized the instructor as a retired deputy chief from the New York City Fire Department who used to go on retreats with my father. This instructor had retired from the job twenty years to the day, and then had gone on to law school and become a lawyer.

He took attendance on the first day of class, and when he got to my name, he said, "Your father is Frank McVey."

"That's right," I said.

"Good man. I knew your dad for many years."

In November, I got my first winter jacket from the fire department. In the past, they had always had red jackets, each with a yellow Maltese cross. This jacket was blue with a white Maltese cross, reading RESCUE on top, and FLORAL PARK on the bottom. The jacket made me feel much more official than when I wore regular civilian clothes, and instilled more confidence in the patients. At home, I put it on the dining room chair and just waited for a call to come over so I could wear it. I was in the living room playing chess with my father when a signal came through for someone having difficulty breathing.

The location was on the way to the firehouse, so I went straight to the call in my car. When I pulled up, I saw that Ed Rothenberg, Kevin

Tholl, and Mike Ostipwko had also all arrived on the scene in their own cars. Together, we went in the front door and into the living room. I heard a gasp. The cops, who had been first on the scene, were carrying the patient from a recliner and laying him on the floor. The patient's wife was panicking. One of the cops reassured her, told her that we were going to work on her husband, and then took her aside and took down information.

Meanwhile, the four of us were checking the patient. Kevin was at the head checking for breathing, while Ed was checking for a carotid pulse. The patient continued to gasp, although he was now unconscious and turning blue. I was next to Kevin trying to feel for a radial pulse. Nothing. Ed shook his head and placed his hands on the man's chest to begin CPR. Since I was still a probie, Kevin grabbed me by my collar and forced me over to the patient's head to do the mouth-to-mouth. I knew there was absolutely no way I was getting out of this one, so I pulled out my handkerchief, put it over the patient's mouth, and forced air from my mouth into the patient's. I did this every fifth compression that Ed was doing. This was the first time I had done mouth-to-mouth for a long time—not since that overdose during the summer. But that time I had breathed into the patient only once, and then got a hold of the resuscitator. This time, I was stuck doing it for a while. It seemed like forever. While I was breathing air into the patient, I heard agonal respirations. The respirations were not enough to sustain him, however, so I kept breathing. I thought I was going to get initiated good this time, thinking about stories of patients vomiting in their rescuers' mouths.

In a weak and shaky voice, I said, "Does anybody have an ambu-bag?"

"The bus is almost here, Dan," Mike Ostipwko said. "Just hang in there."

Finally, the ambulance arrived and someone handed me the resuscitator. Boy, that was a relief. I continued the ventilations using the resuscitator.

They put the patient on the trundle and carried him to the ambulance with CPR in progress. I jumped into the ambulance and got ready, and as soon as the patient was wheeled in, I quickly got on the compressions.

Assistant Chief Ricky Maickels knelt by the patient's head and did ventilations. "Come on, Danny, push harder," he said.

I pushed harder.

Meanwhile, some of the other guys were working on advanced life-support methods, such as administering drugs and communicating with Medical Control. Then at some point, I began feeling tired, so I switched off with someone else to do the compressions. Ricky stayed on ventilations the whole way to the hospital.

We put the patient in the hands of the emergency staff at the hospital. They were still working on him when we left. This time we were not as lucky as the first time I had had done compressions, however, as the patient expired.

This was actually the third time I had done compressions, though, not the second. The day I took the Suffolk Police test, I was returning to town when I saw the ambulance in front of a house. I pulled over and offered help, but Jim McEntee said there was a lot of manpower inside and told me not to go in. It was a cardiac arrest. The wife of the patient was in front of the house crying. A neighbor came over and consoled her.

They carried the patient out of the house, and while they were maneuvering him, stopped CPR for a moment. Paul Abbruzzese told me to get on compressions, so I did. I did the compressions just long enough for them to get the trundle situated, so they could lift him into the ambulance. Since there was so much manpower already, I did not go to the hospital.

After the ambulance took off, I went inside the house to help clean up. This was a rather sad case. The man had been only thirty-eight years old and had kids—and he didn't survive. He was doing work in his attic when it happened. When we were done cleaning up, we needed to know how to shut off the light, and it hit me kind of hard when his son showed me the light switch. He was holding back a sob when he said, "Just pull the string next to the lightbulb."

Some twenty years later, in the fall of 1999, I met the good neighbor that consoled the patient's wife at a church function. We got to talking about the incident, and he said that the wife and kids had just come back from shopping and found him in the attic unconscious.

The following monthly drill had a bad turnout. The only people that showed up were John Bennet, Ricky Maickels, Jim Friedman, and me. John was the first lieutenant at the time. The poor turnout made him kind of unhappy.

"I can't believe these guys," he said. "They get their minimum qualifications and say, 'Hurray, I'm in Rescue!' "

Since we didn't have enough people to hold a drill, John turned it into a pep talk session. He came down on me for backing out of calls, mentioning a call that had happened in May sometime. I had walked into the house and Jim Friedman had been doing mouth-to-mouth on a patient while a police officer was doing compressions.

Jim had said, "We have an arrest. Go outside and tell them to bring everything in."

I had been willing to get involved, but Jim had seemed kind of persistent in telling me to go outside, so I went and waited for the truck to respond. Meanwhile, Assistant Chief Ricky Maickels pulled up, ran back to his trunk, grabbed his equipment, and ran into the house to take over. I explained that all to John, but he told me I had to show more initiative. So I told him about some other arrests that I had worked on.

"That doesn't mean shit," he said. "When you do CPR in most cases, you are only transporting a body to the hospital to be pronounced dead by a doctor. I once saw a guy bleed to death right in front of me. He had badly ulcerated legs, and one of the veins popped, and there he went. You've got to think quickly in these situations, because it can get messy after awhile. You've got to think about how you're going to handle a situation like this. You're going to talk to patients who will arrest right in front of you."

"Also," he added, "I notice you are not too involved in fire calls."

I explained that I used the engine across the street from where I lived to take me to fire calls. John advised me to come to the main firehouse to use my own company truck to go. That way I could get more involved on fire calls.

I thought about what John had said. George Funke from the Active Engine Company had even welcomed me to use his truck to go to fires. The thought was nice, but John was right. I had to show more initiative at fires. I remembered the last time I used the engine to take me to a fire call. It was a working house fire on Verbena Avenue. We pulled up and I saw the house engulfed in flames. I went to the backyard with an engine man, and we were looking for a way into the house to do a search and rescue. There was no way we could enter the house, though, since the fire was too intense. So I didn't do much at that fire. Fortunately, there was nobody home at the time.

While we'd been looking for a way in, though, ex-Captain Tom Slattery had been on his hands and knees by the back door. "Hey, probie, come here," he'd said to me. "I want to show you something."

I went over next to Tom, and he said, "Feel for the floor."

I felt for the floor and found that it was so weak that my hand broke it using minimal strength. There was practically no floor left.

"See that?" Tom said. "Never go into one of these by yourself."

Sometime after that, Garry Gronert told me about a big fire in which he felt for the floor and found there was none. If either Garry or Tom had walked into the situation too fast, they would have fallen down into the basement of a fiery building.

One thing I still remember Garry saying when he told me his story was, "Don't let anyone tell you that you can't get killed in one of these stupid little house fires."

After that drill with John, I made sure that when a fire call came over, I responded with the rescue truck. Shortly thereafter, a call came over as a structure fire at the bus company on Jericho Turnpike. I rushed to the main firehouse where my company was stationed and got on the rescue truck. I geared up and put on a Scott Pack (a self-contained breathing apparatus) on the way there, which was hard to do in a fast-moving truck, but I managed to get it on correctly. We pulled up to the scene and I carried in tools and offered assistance.

Second Lieutenant Paul Abbruzzese took my tools away and said, "Dan, go over there by Reliance." "They need another man on the hose line." Reliance was the name of the engine company that covered the north side of town.

There was a lot of smoke and flames on both floors of the building. This was more than just a routine call. Still, I did what Paul told me and went over to the Reliance men.

Firefighter Gormley was on the nozzle. He asked me, "Do you want to take the nozzle?"

"I better not," I said. "This is my first time going into a big fire."

He was very calm, and I thought it was nice of him to ask me if I wanted to operate the nozzle. "Just relax," he said. "You're going to do all right. When they break the door down, we're going in. When I stop moving, I'm going to aim high toward the ceiling, then you go down low with your part of the hose." (Since the hose is high-pressure, you need three or four men to hold it, so it doesn't get out of control.)

Once the door opened, we went in. Gormley aimed high with the spray for a few seconds and then aimed straight. At this point, the fire darkened down, and the flames disappeared, but there was a lot of smoke. Our oxygen was turned on, so we were breathing clean air. It was still scary, though, because I could not see anything. I just felt Gormley's boot brush against mine every few seconds.

"Are you all right?" I asked periodically.

"I'm all right kid," he'd say. "Just you hang in there."

After Gormley sprayed the big part of the fire out, we waited for the smoke to clear. At this point we were under the supervision of Fred Herbert. I'm not sure, but I think he might have been a lieutenant of the Reliance Company at the time. Reliance's firefighter Slick Watts then chopped the walls apart. When he did, more fire erupted. Gormley sprayed the fire out, while I stood from behind and held the hose down out of his way. It was like an oven in there, but it was a cold day, so I appreciated the heat to some extent.

After a few times chopping through various walls, the smoke started to get lighter. The heat left that part of the building and we were feeling the cold air coming in. Today, we would have had to keep our air tanks on. However, back then, as soon as the air cleared up, we were allowed to take our masks off. I had done well nursing my air. I had positioned myself so I wouldn't breathe too heavily, and still had three-quarters of a tank of air left.

As we continued working, I heard sirens, which meant Reliance had called for mutual aid from another town. By now, our part of the fire was extinguished; however, there was still fire on the second floor. Slick and some other men took another hose upstairs. I wanted to go up, too, since I had a lot of air left in my tank. While I was trying to get involved, another firefighter was poking the ceiling looking for fire. Some of the debris came down and went into his eyes. Assistant Chief Maickels told me to take the firefighter to the rescue truck. I walked him off the fire scene like I was walking a blind man. Several of the men from my company took him to the truck and washed his eyes out. At this point I heard that a few firefighters had already been hospitalized for smoke inhalation and other injuries. That explained the sirens I'd heard while I was inside the burning building.

While they were washing the injured firefighter's eyes out, someone said to me, "Dan, take care of the chief."

Being escorted into the back of the rescue truck was First Assistant Chief John Gehring. He was a little overcome by smoke. I took his blood pressure and wrote out a report. He was all right and didn't have to go to the hospital. I think the firefighter with the eye injury went to the hospital, but was released. Another firefighter named

Richy, from the Hook and Ladder Company, was sitting on a bunk in the truck vomiting. The vomit had black spots, which indicated smoke inhalation. He was therefore transported to the hospital.

Within the next hour, the fire was completely extinguished. We put the equipment back on the trucks and went back to our respective firehouses. Back at our house, we put full air tanks in place of the used ones, while the Hose Company replaced their used hoses with new ones. After we cleaned up and restocked, we went downstairs to the Rescue room and had pizza.

When Richy walked into the Rescue room, he said, "Hey, guys, thanks a lot."

Someone asked, "Want a slice, Rich?"

Richy replied, "Oh God, no thanks. I can't even look at the stuff." Later, Richy had blood gas tests done at the hospital and was sent home.

Sometime that month, there was another fire call at a private residence. Again, I responded with my own company. It was becoming routine to gear up with them and put a Scott Pack on. At the scene, I went into the house with Lieutenant Abbruzzese. As I passed through the living room, it seemed there was nothing wrong. There was no smoke and no fire. When we went upstairs, it became hotter. It was like walking into an oven. The fire was confined to one room. The Engine Company had done a good job preventing the fire from spreading throughout the upstairs.

Abbruzzese and I did a search and rescue and found no victims. Like the fire at the bus company, the engine men were chopping down walls to get to the fire inside the structure, to prevent rekindling. I didn't get to do any firefighting since my job at this call was search and rescue.

Later on, well into December, although winter wasn't officially here yet, I went to the firehouse to hang out. Ed Rothenberg, Louie Mancuso, and Paul Abbruzzese showed up for Christmas caroling. No, we didn't go around the neighborhood singing Christmas songs.

You could never get me to do that. Instead, we rode the truck around various neighborhoods playing Christmas songs on a cassette player through the PA system. The only question left was, Who's going to be Santa Clause? I was one hundred and twenty pounds at the time so I thought it certainly wouldn't be me. Ed and Louie were lightweights also. Paul was a little heavyset, but he wanted to drive the truck.

Then I heard someone say, "Danny is the probie, so let's make him be Santa Clause."

They used a pillow to make me look fat, and Ed was helping me fix the pillow in place by tightening my belt around it. I must have been moving around too much because Ed said, "Stand still, damn it."

"Since you're yelling at me," I told him "you're not getting anything for Christmas."

"Screw you, Santa," he said.

As we made our rounds in the neighborhood, I was beginning to like the Santa job. Kids are so innocent. They really believed that I was the real Santa Clause.

One kid asked me if I would get him a particular toy, and his mother told him, "Yes, he's bringing it on Christmas."

We rode around town until it got dark. Then we stopped at Louie's house and met his family.

After we left, I asked Louie, "How old is your sister?"

"Fifteen," he replied.

"She's cute," I said.

"Now, now, be nice. That's my kid sister."

Next, we stopped at Jim Friedman's house. His wife had had a baby girl over the summer. I went into the kitchen and saw her sitting in a baby seat. She was getting so big, she was able to hold her own baby bottle.

We left Jim's house and rode to the other side of town to see Paul Dombrowski's son who had been born over the summer also.

As I walked into his house, his wife said, "That's a cute Santa."

They sat me on a chair and had me hold the baby and pose for a picture.

Finally, we visited Archie Cheng's house. Archie was a new member who'd joined the company in November. He and his wife also had a baby boy who was about three months old at that time.

Later on that month, we had a rescue call inside Floral Park Memorial High School. The call came over as a possible overdose. One thing I never got used to was seeing a teenager do something self-destructive. Upon our arrival, they called for the trundle. I wheeled the trundle into the hallway and came upon the patient, who was covered in vomit. Officer Gallo was the cop assigned to the case. He was talking to one of the patient's friends, trying to find out if the boy had taken anything else besides booze. He assured the friend that he wasn't looking to arrest anyone but needed to know if the patient took any drugs so he could order the proper treatment. Meanwhile, the patient was being placed in the bus and taken to the hospital.

Chief Jim Fairben was the chief in charge of the call. He gave me a ride in the chief's car back to the firehouse. Sitting in the front passenger seat was his lady friend, Liz. She asked how the kid was.

"He'll be okay," Jim said. "It seems like he only took booze. He's going to have some hangover when he wakes up tomorrow, that's for sure. Tonight he overdosed on Jack Daniels and tomorrow we'll get a call on him for an overdose of tomato juice and aspirin."

A few days after this call we were summoned back to the same school to aid a student who had passed out. The first thing I thought was that it was another overdose. I went to the firehouse and responded with the ambulance. Pete Walters was driving and I was riding shotgun. As we were riding down the street with the sirens blaring,

Pete was humming to himself, as calm as could be. I looked at him and figured I should be the same way—calm and collected.

As we pulled up, they were asking for the trundle to be taken to the nurse's office. I walked into the nurse's office with the trundle and saw a teenage girl with an oxygen mask on. The cop on the scene was asking her how old she was, to which she replied, "Fourteen." The story was that the school was having its Christmas concert that night and the girl had passed out while singing in the chorus. I was glad to see that it was not another overdose. She didn't seem like the kind of kid who was into drugs and alcohol.

Her mother came over after we placed her on the trundle, and said, "Let these guys take care of you, and I'll meet you at the hospital." She then patted her daughter on the head and said, "I love you."

I was the EMT who rode in the back on the way to the hospital. Pete drove, and Louie Mancuso rode up front with him. The girl was able to talk and didn't report being in much distress, except that she complained of general weakness. I kept her on oxygen until we arrived at the hospital. She told me that she was just getting over the flu and was on medication, and that she hadn't eaten anything because she'd been afraid it would make her sick. That explained why she passed out. She was able to have a sense of humor.

When we pulled her out of the ambulance at the emergency room, she laughed and said, "Don't drop me."

I said, "Don't worry. We haven't dropped anybody yet this week."

On the way back from the hospital, Lou teased me about being in the back of the ambulance with the young girl. "You were a little sweet on her," he said. "I know you. You had your eyes on my little sister."

After that call, I had two weeks off from college for Christmas break. The thing I didn't like about that break was knowing that I would have to go back after the new year for another week of classes and a week of finals. For the Christmas break, my parents and I flew to Michigan. My niece was sick on Christmas Eve. The next day, on

Christmas, my nephew—her brother—had the same attack of the stomach flu. My brother-in-law's other niece was on antibiotics and just getting over the flu. Sure enough, there was something going around. I was lucky I never caught the bug. However, I easily caught the common cold from my sister's kids. Every time I was around them when they had a cold, I would surely catch it.

I was back in New York by New Year's Eve. That night, Marc Krauss and I went to two parties. The first was in Stewart Manor. We found the place a little early. We were told to show up around 11:00, and it was around 10:30 or so, so we didn't want to go in right away. We sat in Marc's car listening to the country music station 1050 WHN on the AM dial, waiting for the party to start. We listened to songs we'd heard throughout the old year, such as "Where Do I Put Her Memory?" by Charley Pride, "Crazy Love" by Poco, and others.

At around 11:00, we went up to the front door of the house. A young lady let us in. We stayed for about an hour and a half. When the ball dropped, everyone went around wishing each other a happy New Year. We left that party and went to the other one, where we drank and mingled. The first party had been mostly girls, but the second was mostly guys. After we left the second party, we stopped at the main firehouse and saw the end of the Hook and Ladder Company's annual New Year's party.

It was the start of another year. My goal was to use my skills to make a good impression on the rest of the Rescue Company. I went back to school for my week of classes and week of finals, and then we had two weeks off for the mid-year break.

It was the second Wednesday in January. I had taken my last final that day, and knew it was my drill night. In fact, I forgot about plans to go out with Marc because drill was more important to me. My parents were away in Florida at the time.

When I was getting ready to fix my dinner, I heard the doorbell ring. Marc was at the door.

"Come on, we're going out, remember?" he said.

"We have a drill tonight," I said.

"Forget the drill." Marc physically pushed me out of my own house and into his car.

I was annoyed at him. It wasn't the first time he'd made plans on the night of a Rescue meeting or drill. I wanted to let him know that this was the last time he was going to pull this trick on me, so I acted nasty toward him. He got insulted and drove back to my house.

"Get lost," he said.

I told him that I was sorry I messed up his plans.

"Just get lost," he repeated.

I left the car, walked back to my house, and fixed my dinner. I wasn't going to start off the New Year by missing a drill. I was sorry about the way I'd talked to him, but the drill was more important to me than going out and having a good time.

After I ate dinner, I went to the firehouse. The topic of the drill was electrical hazards. It was too cold to have an outdoor drill, so we had it in the company room. After the drill, I went home. It felt good to get the year off to a good start by getting credit for a drill. I went to bed not expecting what would happen first thing in the morning.

I was awakened by the telephone at around 7:30 in the morning. I wasn't happy about it; it was the first day in awhile that I could sleep late.

It was Marc. "Look, Dan, I'm really sick and I need you to drive me around on my job today. I had a migraine attack."

"Okay, Marc, I'll be right over."

"Just come over like you're going to a rescue call," he said, "Don't take a shower or anything."

After I hung up, I had a quick cup of coffee and drove to his house. I picked him up and then drove him around on his job. He apologized to me about the night before. After I took him on his rounds, I dropped him home where he was to nurse his migraine.

Later on that evening, I went to the firehouse to hang out. I saw Marc's father, Hank.

"How's Marc?" I asked.

"He's feeling much better, Dan. Thank you for driving him around today."

I went home early that night since I had to catch a plane the next morning to meet my parents in Florida.

The next day I arrived in St. Petersberg Beach. We stayed there for a week, and then drove to Boca Raton to see my other sister and her family.

The New Ambulance

We had been waiting for this day for a long time. Assistant Chief Ricky Maickels was like an expectant father.

Marc stopped by at my house unexpectedly to announce the news. "Hey, Dan. Your new toy is in the firehouse."

We went to the firehouse to look at the new delivery. We had been renting a white and orange ambulance over the summer. Now we had our own red and white ambulance with silver lettering. Sure enough, there was Ricky Maickels in the back checking things out. He had served on the Ambulance Committee for many years.

That same night, the new bus was put into service. I still remember the first call I responded to on it. It was a person with difficulty breathing, and I rode in the back with the patient to the hospital.

Sometime in March was the dedication for this new vehicle. We had a ceremony in front of the firehouse, and the mayor broke a bottle of champaign on the front wheel. This event in which we baptized the vehicle was known as the wet-down. I met a lot of old-timers who had been invited to the event. These guys were no longer in the company because they had moved out of town or had other commitments. I remembered some of them, when I was a kid, chasing fire trucks.

Some firemen from New Hyde Park came to the event to hose us down as a joke. Our guys put gear on and went back at them. I saw Mike Ostipwko wrestling with one of the guys, trying to gain control of the hose. Meanwhile, Marc Krauss decided to join in the fun. He pulled the alert truck out of the barn and was going to hook up a hose to a hydrant. It was too bad for him that the fun was already over. The men from New Hyde Park were already going back.

When the ambulance was still new to us, we had a call at the Tulip Avenue Apartments. I remember it to this day. It came over as a patient with difficulty breathing. Mike Ostipwko, Garry Gronert, and I went into the apartment. There was an elderly lady standing and leaning on a chair. She said she felt comfortable in that position, or, should I say, less uncomfortable. She was really having a hard time. She and her husband both informed us that she had had the flu since Palm Sunday. Gary checked for leg edema and found her legs full of fluid. He checked her lung fields and found them full of fluid also. Then he looked at her arms for a vein.

He said to the patient, whose name was Enrica, "When we get you into the ambulance, I'm going to try to give you a needle to make you feel better."

We put her on oxygen, sat her in the stair chair, and carried her down the stairs. Mike and Garry were doing the carrying, and I held the oxygen. As they turned on the landing, I saw that the patient was turning blue.

"Enrica!" Mike exclaimed. There was no answer. I was shocked. She had just been talking to us a minute ago inside the apartment.

When they got her to the bottom of the stairs, Mike and Garry quickly put her on the trundle and placed the CPR board behind her back. They checked her pulse and respirations, and found no pulse or breathing. They began CPR. The cop on the scene radioed the dispatcher to send out a second call for a cardiac arrest.

After a few sequences of CPR, I heard Mike say, "Enrica, you back with us?"

He found a pulse and saw signs of respiration. We quickly wheeled her into the ambulance. We hooked her up to the EKG monitor. She had a very slow heart rate, which is known as bradycardia, but it slowly climbed back to a more normal rate. Kevin Tholl had heard the second call for a cardiac arrest and had responded to the scene in his car. He now jumped into the ambulance and read the EKG strip.

"Boy, she must go to church every Sunday," he said. In other words, she was lucky to still be alive.

We took her to the hospital with Mike constantly talking to her.

As she was still unconscious, this ended up being a form of what is known as psychological first aid. When we left the emergency room to go home, she was still alive.

As we were all leaving to go home, Mike said, "Good call, guys."

Quite a few years later, we were called back to the same apartment for a routine non-life-threatening emergency. There was Enrica walking around. She had had a few friends over, and one of them was the patient. If I remember correctly, this person signed a form to refuse further medical aid.

It felt good to see Enrica up walking around, however, and listening to her tell us how great we were, even though I didn't personally participate in the CPR process that had saved her life.

That call with Enrica was the first spectacular save that I saw in the new ambulance.

Spring of 1980

It was that time of year again. Jim Fairben was to go out as ex-chief, and his staff all moved up, with John Gehring becoming the new chief. Our man Ricky Maickels became third assistant chief while Jim's brother, Kenny Fairben, became fourth assistant chief.

After the chief elections, we had refreshments. On line for the food was Fred Herbert. He sure loved his food.

When he saw me, he said, "There's my firefighting partner." He was referring to the big fire at the bus company on Jericho Turnpike, the one in which I had worked with Reliance Company.

"All I did was hold the hose and chop some walls apart," I replied.

Fred said, "You did what you were told and you did a *good* job. You come into a fire with me and you'll learn."

He was right about that. I learned more about fighting fire with Fred in those few hours than I'd learned in eight sessions in fire school. Another good thing about working with Fred was that he hadn't acted like he was the only firefighter who could put the fire out.

A few weeks later, we had the installation dinner at Plattdeutsche Park in Franklin Square. We had the usual ceremony, with the installation of the officers and staff, followed by food and dancing.

The thing I remember about that installation dinner was the ending. There was a party downstairs where a woman was having an epileptic seizure. A man came up, saw us in our uniforms, and told us about the situation. Kevin Tholl went to call an ambulance. Meanwhile, the new fourth assistant chief, Kenny Fairben, and I went downstairs into the party room, and saw an unconscious woman in a postdictal stage of seizure. That stage is when the patient stops convulsing and goes into a deep sleep. I checked the airway and saw that she was breathing.

Kenny wrapped some ice in a napkin and gave it to me, saying, "Put this behind her neck."

I placed it behind the woman's neck. This treatment was to lessen the likelihood of another seizure happening.

Kevin's sister-in-law, Claudia, then arrived. She was a nurse. She talked to the patient, who was, by this time, slipping in and out of consciousness. The three of us just stayed with her and monitored her vital signs, while Claudia kept talking to her. Meanwhile, the Franklin Square Fire Department showed up. We had to leave and let them take over. By that time, she had started convulsing again. The EMT from the ambulance that had responded put a bite stick between her teeth—a method that is now outdated as, subsequent to this incident, it was removed as protocol by the health department.

When I went upstairs, I saw that Claudia was upset about the woman. Who knew? Maybe if we'd let her stay, since she was a woman helping another woman, it would have prevented the second seizure from occurring. It was a tough judgment call.

In May of that year, I responded with the ambulance to a call for an unconscious female. I walked in the house, which was crowded with members from Rescue, since it was after work hours, and saw a woman lying on the floor. She was turning blue and there was no pulse.

Ricky Maickels yelled, "Get on her!" and CPR was immediately started. Ronnie Nahas attempted to insert an esophageal gastric tube airway into her.

When they were carrying her out, I ran into the back of the ambulance to begin CPR as soon as she was wheeled in, until I heard someone yell, "Danny, get out!" I didn't like the order. However, since it was from someone with rank, I obeyed and planned to complain about it later.

The ambulance took off to the hospital and I went back to the firehouse. I had been told by my officers to show initiative and that is what I had done at this call. That officer had had no right to tell me to leave and then, on a later day, say that I had backed out of the call. I could understand if the problem was that there was another member with little experience in the back of the truck, as they didn't want two newer members on the same call. But, after telling me to leave, they'd better not say later that I "backed out." This is just what had happened on a call about a year before, and I had been so mad.

Then, to add assault to injury, when the ambulance returned, I heard the crew talking happily about how the patient was brought back to consciousness. I was feeling kind of jealous I guess.

A day or two later, when I cooled off, I approached Captain Mike Ostipwko and told him about the situation. Since he is the one who did evaluations of all the members, he was the one to talk to. He listened and was nice about it. I guess he must have ironed the problem out, too, because I didn't have any of trouble after that. This was around the same time when my confidence was starting to blossom.

Unfortunately, the patient died in the hospital a day or two after the call, despite the efforts to bring her heart back in the ambulance.

It was still May, and the closing of the spring semester. My parents were away in Michigan for my nephew's first communion, and I had the house to myself. One morning, I remember the alarm going off to get me up for classes. I meant to hit the snooze button, hit the button to shut off the alarm instead. Of course, I overslept. When I awoke it was 9:30—the time my class was supposed to start.

I said, "The hell with it" and just played hooky that day.

Sometime later, while my parents were still in Michigan, I got a call in the middle of the night. It was a rude awakening. Kenny Fairben was a police dispatcher for his regular job, and I heard his voice on the radio say, "Be advised; full arrest."

I drove past the firehouse and saw that the ambulance was long gone. Therefore, I drove directly to the scene. Kenny's radio announcement must have been the second call for manpower because the patient was already in the ambulance being worked on. Apparently, I had slept through the initial tone.

Doctor Larry Shivers was on the scene, working on him and ordering our guys to administer whatever medication and defibrillation was necessary. Then he stepped out of the ambulance and said there was nothing more he could do. He ordered just to transport and continue CPR. The patient was pronounced dead at the hospital. I remembered Doctor Shivers from when I was about ten years old. Whenever I was a kid and saw a rescue call, he would be there. You will not find doctors that make those kinds of house calls today. Now, ambulance protocols have been enhanced so that more advanced life support can be administered, lessening the need for doctors on the scene. For example, in 1976, the Rescue Company got its first telemetry, in which communications can be established with a doctor at Medical Control.

In any event, I went home after this call. The next day, I fixed the house up because my sister and brother-in-law would be flying in from Michigan for my sister's ten-year reunion for nursing school. My parents would be staying at their place to babysit the kids.

While she was at the reunion, my brother-in-law, Larry, and I went out to dinner. I remember him asking me about what I was going to do when I graduated from college. I told him I needed three more classes to graduate, so I had extended my college career into the fall semester of 1980. After we ate, we went back home and watched television. Larry lay on the couch and I was stretched out on the love seat. I was so tired, I don't remember what we were watching. I just lay back and kept dozing off. I remember Larry being kind of sleepy too. We would almost doze off at the same time and then wake up simultaneously. Finally, we decided that we could stay awake no longer, so we went to bed for the night.

A few weeks later, my other sister and brother-in-law drove up from Florida for a visit. By this time, my parents were back and my other sister had returned to Michigan. Karen and Frank, my sister and brother-in-law from Florida, brought the kids with them. I remember them pulling in the driveway with buckets of Kentucky

Fried Chicken. They were absolutely starving from the long ride they had taken to see us.

One hot day while they were in town, I was mowing my lawn, and I was just getting done with the backyard and on my way to do the front when the alarm sounded a 22. That meant it was a Signal 9 rescue call.

My sister came out and gave me some kind of signal, since I could not hear her above the lawn mower. I turned off the mower and she said, "Two-oh-five, Floral Boulevard." I immediately got in my car and drove to the address.

When I got there, I realized something was wrong. There were no police cars at the house, and the police usually got to the scene before we did. My sister must have given me the wrong address. You had to be careful to be sure of the right address. Take Cisney Street and Cypress Street—one of our members once got confused and responded to the other street. There was a call on Cisney and he responded to Cypress by mistake. I assumed it must have been 205 Floral *Parkway,* not *Boulevard,* so I responded to the firehouse and jumped on the rescue truck. My Floral Parkway assumption was also wrong. The correct location of the call was actually on Floral Boulevard, but the number was 250, not 205.

The ambulance was out of service, so Louie Marcus drove the truck to the scene with me riding shotgun. It was a good thing that I responded because it was early in the afternoon on a workday, and we were shorthanded. It was a routine call for a sick elderly man. All we could do was work up a set of vital signs and give him first aid. He had a fever, so I put a cold, damp cloth on his head. We called for mutual aid from New Hyde Park Fire Department for an ambulance and they responded. When they left to take him to the hospital, we were released from the scene.

After this call, I went back home. Cathy, one of my sister's childhood friends, came over with her daughter, and we all sat and talked about childhood fun times. Cathy's daughter played with my niece and nephew.

Another night while they were still in town, Karen and Frank wanted to take me to a movie. The movie we decided to see was *The Changeling*, with George C. Scott. It was some kind of horror movie similar to *Amityville Horror*. George C. Scott lived in a mansion that was haunted by a ghost of a boy who once lived in the big house and was murdered by his father. It turned out that the boy's father drowned him in the bathtub.

Another event we did that week was something my father had been waiting for: we took my niece to see Sandy Duncan as Peter Pan in the musical production. We couldn't take my nephew, since he was too young at the time, so it was just my sister, brother-in-law, niece, father, and I. We took the Long Island Railroad into Manhattan, and stopped to have lunch at a place that my father liked, only to find it closed for renovations. So we went to another restaurant close by. After eating, we went to the theater to see *Peter Pan*. Sandy Duncan was amazing. She was so relaxed flying around the whole theater. It was hard to see the strings that were holding her up so high. While she was flying, all of the kids in the theater were cheering.

After the show, we took a subway back to Penn Station. We had to board a car that was hot and standing-room-only, since it was rush hour. One man who was sitting down looked like he was about to have a panic attack. It was very hot, with no air-conditioning, and he was sweating and looked nervous. He tried to give his seat to my sister.

"Would you like to sit down?" he asked her.

"No, that's all right," she replied.

He sat back down when the train pulled away and started to relax. I guessed he had a little claustrophobia being on the crowded train. I was hoping that I was not going to have to put my EMT skills to work, and I realized I was feeling the way Marc Krauss said that he always felt. He said he felt like the guardian angel every time he was in a movie theater, restaurant, or any public place. In other words, we felt responsible if something didn't go right.

Anyway, that night, we made it home with no mishaps. We got off at the Bellerose Station near my house and my mother and nephew were there to meet us.

Soon after, Frankie, my nephew, did something mean to Tracy, my niece. I forget what it was. Tracy went up to him and Frankie pushed her away or something like that. Frankie was two and Tracy was almost five at the time.

"That was mean," I told Frankie. "You should tell Tracy you're sorry."

He reluctantly and very slowly walked toward Tracy.

"Go on," I said, "tell her you're sorry."

He slowly continued. When he got close enough to her, he put his arms around her and hugged her.

When we got home, my mother said it looked like some bad news had come in the mail. I had failed my computer course that spring semester. I was disappointed, of course, and was wondering whether I should take it over in the fall or summer. I called the college and they said that the course was being offered in the summer. Plus, if I took it in the fall, then I would have an extra course to worry about. The course in the summer was held for just three hours on Saturdays, which also meant my whole summer wasn't shot, because I would still have the rest of the week off. So I signed up for the class in the summer.

Karen talked to me later on that evening. We were in the basement. She said, encouragingly, "Danny, you have a second chance to make this course up in the summer. I know a guy that was just diagnosed with terminal cancer. He doesn't have a second chance."

Then we got talking about my being in the fire department. "I'm really proud of what you are doing, but you should get into something else on the side—like bowling, for instance," she told me. "I'm telling you this because eventually you're going to find yourself getting depressed. I know how that is from nursing. I know you like the Rescue Company. You're actually saving people's lives.... "

I brought up the lady who'd died in front of me almost a year before, and she said, "This is what I mean about getting depressed."

She was right, although I didn't really learn what she meant until many years later. At this time, my confidence was improving and I was raring to go. I thought that since I was getting used to being around sick and injured people that it meant things didn't bother me. I was willing to get my hands dirty and be able to laugh about it. But, the truth was that anybody who thought this job didn't bother them was fooling himself. It wouldn't be until many years later that I found that out.

In my first computer class that summer, the professor explained the mathematics of basic computer language. I was finally grasping it, but I also immediately signed up for tutoring. My tutor was a student majoring in computers. In my first session with the tutor, I showed him my completed homework assignment, and he said it was perfect.

"It's almost like you don't even need tutoring," he said. "You seem to know what you're doing, but you're just not sure of yourself."

The previous spring semester when I'd taken the class, it had seemed impossible. However, in the summer class, it seemed as easy as basic arithmetic. I told my tutor whom my professor was that spring, and he said, "Oh, yes, I know him real well. He's the one who knows how to make simple arithmetic look like calculus."

My final grade at the end of the course was a solid *B*.

Summer of 1980

In the early 1960s, our town opened up the village swimming pool. It was a nice place for kids and families to go on hot summer days. I belonged to the pool almost every summer while growing up. The summer of 1980 was no exception. I could not go then as much as I had in high school, however, because I was busy with the fire department. In fact, that was a brutal summer for the fire department.

I did make it to the pool a few times that year though. One day we were summoned to the pool for a child with convulsions. I arrived with the ambulance. It was a little girl about seven or eight years old. We wheeled her from the first-aid station to the ambulance, and I stayed in the back with her. She was in an unconscious state, which is normal after a convulsion. While en route to the hospital, I kept a bite stick close by, just in case. I placed a cold compress behind her neck to prevent reoccurrence of the convulsion. We made it to the hospital all right. We left her with the emergency department and went home. Pete Walters, while writing up the paperwork for that call, said, "Nice work, Dan."

Another pool call happened while Assistant Chief Kenny Fairben was with his then three-year-old son Keith. The call was for a little boy of about four years old, and it was a head injury. Kenny was really good with the kid. He kept talking to him, while the child's mother was sitting on the trundle holding her son.

Another day I decided to go swimming at the pool. It was a very hot day and I just had to take a swim. While at the pool, I heard the horns sound a 22, but I figured that I was not available to respond. This was my free time and my average on making calls was more than sufficient. Well, I did not get out of it so easily. While I was walking toward the pool to take a swim, I saw a crowd of people by the diving boards.

Paul Sangen, a prospective member of the Alert Engine Company at the time, approached me and said, "Dan, that rescue call is for a kid who fell off the diving board. It's all yours."

I rushed over to the victim. The lifeguards were performing first aid. They were doing a good job, so I let them continue with their thing, but I told them I was from Rescue. One of them moved over, so I could kneel by the kid's head. He was conscious and breathing. He was able to talk to me and said that his shoulder was hurt. I asked him if he had hit his head and he replied that he had not. He was a good kid, able to talk and laugh with me. It felt good to know that he was well enough that he could keep a sense of humor. He wasn't in much pain. The lifeguards put a sling and a swathe around his shoulder, which minimized the pain.

When Rescue arrived, Harry White walked over and kidded around with the patient, saying, "You were supposed to jump in the water, not on the concrete."

The kid laughed. He seemed to get a little apprehensive, however, when I took his blood pressure. When I was finished, he looked at me nervously and said, "Am I going to be all right?"

I reassured him that it was normal to take the vital signs of every patient, no matter how little the emergency. He seemed to relax again.

They took him to the hospital. I did not go with them on the trip; however, after this call I met the kid a few times.

Every time he saw me, he would say, "You're the guy from the emergency that was with me when I got hurt at the pool." He thanked me several times after that. The kid was surely appreciative.

Another memorable event that summer was the department picnic. It was held at the Manorhaven Park on the north shore. It was a good way of bringing the whole department together. I helped set the place up in the morning. I went to the firehouse and helped carry hamburger and hot dog rolls upstairs to be taken to the picnic site. About ten to twenty of us were setting up. As the day started growing hotter, a few of us went back to the firehouse in Hugo

Berta's car to get more stuff. By the time we got back to Manorhaven, the crowd had started to show up. Once our work was done, we started mingling with people and participating.

I spent time talking to Rickie Maickels while he watched his kids play by the water. I remember Rickie telling his kids to stay away from the water, which was kind of polluted. It was the last time we were to have a picnic at that location.

The temperature was well into the nineties and very uncomfortable. Someone had set up a volleyball net and some of the people were now playing volleyball. I didn't play because it was way too hot. I just hung out where it was shady. There was a softball game going on, too, and I heard that Garry Gronert was having heat stroke. It turned out to be an exaggerated rumor, because when I saw him he was all right. He had just been drinking water and putting ice packs under his armpits to cool off. He was able to stay at the picnic; he just had to stop playing ball.

Some cops from the Nassau County Police Sixth Precinct who showed up said the day was so hot that you couldn't enjoy it. I went over to where some of the Rescue Company people were sitting, and the mothers were wetting their babies down with water. The babies were kind of cranky because of the heat. They were Paul Dombrowski's baby son, Archie Cheng's baby son, and Jim Friedman's baby girl, Rebecca. Rebecca was eating chopped up fruit and it was all over her face.

I remember Jim saying, "Be careful, Rebecca, some of it is getting in your mouth."

His baby seemed good, but Paul and Archie's babies were crying a lot because of the heat. Later on, we learned that there was a pool where we could swim if we paid a small fee. I went over to my car and got my bathing suit and towel. Like a fool, I was wearing long blue jeans when I should have been wearing shorts. I got dressed to go swimming. When I got into the pool, I saw some of our guys from Rescue. Paul and Archie's wives were also there, holding their once crying babies. Now in the pool, the babies seemed happy. The cutest thing was that the babies were laughing when their mothers dipped them into the water. The mothers stretched out their arms while holding their splashing babies and the babies hugged each other. That pool saved a lot of us from the heat that day.

It was not the cleanest place to have a picnic, however, so we didn't have any more there. The next year, we had the picnic back at Eisenhower Park.

Going to fire school was a little of both work and play for me. One night, I was invited to go to fire school for a firefighting class. It was a Hook and Ladder course. The Hook and Ladder Company was loaned an old ladder truck from the Huntington Manor Fire Department, and they were to get a brand new truck to replace it in the summer of 1981. Dick Kosinski, of the Truck Company, drove this old truck with Rich Crecenti and me on board. They were sitting in the cab while I sat on the ladder and held on for dear life. When we arrived at the academy in Bethpage, we met Marc Krauss and Buddy Klahn. Richie, Marc, and Buddy were all from the Alert Engine Company. Dick was from the Truck Company, and I from Rescue. We were working with an Engine Company from Hicksville.

The first fire they set, the engine guys put it out pretty fast. I went in to do a search and rescue. I saw a silhouette of a fireman opening a window. It was Marc. When the drill was over, we gathered outside for a critical discussion with the chief instructor. After the discussion, the instructor started another fire, this time in the cellar. He decided to test the guys from Floral Park, so he told me to go and work with the Hicksville firemen. We went into the cellar and put the fire out. There was no place for the water to go so the basement flooded, and the water soaked my turnout coat. My pants were wet and smelled like the gasoline that had been used to start the fire. In any event, the guys from our department did their job well.

When it was all over, they asked, "Where's Danny?" At that point, I was brought out of the basement by the chief instructor.

Buddy said, "There he is. I guess he decided to go swimming. Look at him. He's all wet." Then he turned to me. "You Rescue guys go swimming just when there's work to be done."

He was kidding around, of course, but the thing I learned from him was to communicate my transfer of assignment with the guys from my department. I had not done that, and so they'd thought I was hurt somewhere. After the second fire, we cleaned up and went back home.

Another memorable event that summer was a parade in Suffolk County. I don't remember where in Suffolk. Most parades I marched in were in Nassau County. Eddie Rodriguez of the Alert Engine Company drove me and about two other people to the parade. He had a scanner with the Suffolk County Fire Department, and I learned their radio signals were a little different from ours. Signal 13 to us meant to return to headquarters, for example, while in Suffolk, it meant a working fire was in progress.

When I arrived at the parade site, I ran into Marc Krauss. We hung out while we were waiting for our turn to step off and march. A lot of our guys were drinking too much and acting stupid. One clown pulled down his pants and showed his underwear.

Marc was annoyed, saying, "Doesn't that make you proud to be a fireman?" He and I were kind of conservative about these things and the guys were really getting obnoxious.

I think it was because we had to wait so long until it was our turn to step off and march. Usually, it was sunny out from the time we stepped off until the final steps of the parade. This time when we were lining up to march, there was very little daylight left. Marc and I were sitting in front in the chief's car, which Marc was driving. Marc's father, ex-Chief Hank Krauss, along with Chief John Gehring, was sitting in the back. The fire trucks were behind us, and we were driving behind all the others, who were marching—or, rather, staggering. I thought it was hilarious, but Marc had a lot to say about that.

Finally, his father scolded him, saying, "Would you just worry about your job and forget what those assholes are doing!"

During the parade, a woman spectator was yelling out to us, "Chief! Chief!" and clapping all the while.

When the parade was over, we picked the chief's wife up and went to a Chinese restaurant. I remember that I had egg fu yung. When the bill came, I pulled my wallet out.

"Put that away," Hank said. "Your money is no good here." He then insisted that he would take care of me that night.

I remember another parade that summer. I'm not sure where it was. I know it wasn't the Suffolk parade, though, because it was earlier in the evening. I got home, took my uniform off, and put on my civilian clothes. Two rescue calls came over at the same time. I rushed to the firehouse, but the ambulance was already gone to one of the calls. So I jumped on the rescue truck and responded to the other call. They were both cardiac arrests.

The chief called for mutual aid from New Hyde Park for an ambulance to respond to the second call. When I arrived there, I walked into the house and there was a man on the floor in full cardiac arrest. Joe Oswald was doing the CPR compressions, while Pete Feehan was operating the resuscitator. The man began to vomit all over Pete. For a split second, I remembered the work that Ed Fry and Noel Beebe had done on the woman the summer before. I grabbed the suction unit and suctioned the patient's airway to clear it of vomit. Pete continued with ventilations and I stayed by him with the suction unit. Meanwhile, New Hyde Park showed up. They hooked up the EKG and communicated with Medical Control from inside the house. We then packaged the patient on the trundle and carried him to the ambulance. In the back, the New Hide Park firemen continued to work on him.

As they pulled away, I was standing next to Joe Oswald, and I said to him, "Hey, Joe, you did nice work."

He said, "You think so?"

"You did something and you tried," I said.

While I was walking back to the truck, he said, "Thanks, Dan."

I later learned that the first call had been for a woman in cardiac arrest. The patients from both calls were pronounced dead upon their arrivals at the hospital.

There were two more calls that were kind of disappointing to me that summer. One was early in the morning. When I got to the firehouse the ambulance was gone, so I responded to the scene in my car. When I got there, I asked if they needed any more manpower in the house.

The chief said, "No, they are almost ready to come out with him, and they have enough inside."

So I just hung outside with the chiefs and some of the other members who were not needed in the house. It was early morning, and I was only awake because of the call. As I was rubbing my eyes, Assistant Chief John Billardello tapped me on my cheek and kept saying, "Wake up, wake up!"

Meanwhile, they were carrying out the patient. He was starting to turn blue and I heard him gasping. He was possibly going into cardiac arrest, and I knew I had to act quickly. I jumped into the back of the ambulance, got the resuscitator ready, and started the ventilations immediately after he was wheeled into the bus. Someone else was on compressions. On the way to the hospital, the patient started breathing again and tried to sit up. We told him to lie back down, and Rickie Maickels elevated the head of the stretcher so that any fluid coming up from the lungs would not suffocate the patient. The whole way, the patient was slipping in and out of consciousness. When we arrived at the hospital, the patient tried to sit up again.

"You are doing fine, guy," Ricky told him, and then we wheeled him into the emergency room.

When I got home, I told my father that we had saved a man from cardiac arrest and that after we'd brought him back, he was almost sitting up talking to us.

"You guys do really nice work," he said.

Unfortunately, I found out that the patient died in the hospital that day. I was so mad about that. Here was this person almost sitting up, talking to us after being revived from a full arrest, and he died.

The other disappointing call we had was on the north side of town near where Ed Fry lived. He was already at the scene when we arrived in the ambulance. It was an unconscious woman lying in the bathroom. The police had oxygen on her. She was breathing and did, in fact, have a pulse. We put her on the Reeves stretcher and then carried her out to the trundle, which was in the living room near the front door. We then put her in the ambulance and took off. I remember Ed Fry being in the back of the ambulance with me during the trip.

The patient regained consciousness on the way to the hospital. She was even smiling at us. That was a good sign that she was recovering. She was unable to speak and one side of her body was paralyzed. A little while later, the paralysis went away. I checked her neurological functioning again and it had improved. However, she was still unable to speak. According to Ed Fry, who knew this woman as his neighbor, this was not normal. He said that she normally was able to speak. Despite the woman's illness, I saw that she did have a sense of humor. She was still smiling at us when we arrived at the emergency room. We left her in the hands of the hospital staff, thinking she would be all right.

Either later on that day or the next day, Ed told me the bad news about his neighbor. She had passed away in the hospital. Ed was kind of surprised about it.

"When I saw her regain consciousness and the strength on her weak side came back," he said, "I thought she was going to be all right.

A few days later, apparently the day of this woman's funeral, we were summoned to a street location in the same area where she had lived. It came over as an unconscious female, and they mentioned over the radio that firemen Fry and Gronert were both at the scene. The patient ended up being the daughter of the woman who had died. She was not in a life-threatening condition, but had overdosed on alcohol and was covered in vomit. One thing about an alcohol overdose is that if the person vomits, all of the poison is evacuated from the body. So we knew she was all right.

Her father was there, trying to hold her up, and someone from the company said something to him like "Get out of the way."

Then I heard him say, "I just want to do something."

After that call, Ed announced that he was appalled at the way some of our guys were talking negatively to and about the woman's father. "He was only acting that way," he said, "because he had just lost his wife and then his daughter was sick."

Another shocking day that summer started off as routinely as any other day. It was the beginning of August. Early that afternoon, I went to Jericho Turnpike to get my haircut at the Mainline Beauty Salon and then went home. The day was going as usual until I heard the radio tones go off. I went to the stairway so I could hear the message come over because the radio was in my upstairs bedroom. Police Officer John Kujawa was giving the message. The location he gave was Florence Avenue and Carnation Avenue for a shot man. I responded to the firehouse in my car. At the corner of Floral Boulevard and Carnation Avenue, I saw Venard Brooks. He had just joined the Alert Engine Company the previous April.

"Danny, they're gone," he said. "Just respond to the scene."

I made a left turn on Carnation Avenue and parked my car where the action was. The incident was not on Florence Avenue, as announced. It was one block south of Florence, on Adelaide. I walked over to assist. I saw a crowd of fire department personnel around a man in the street who was bleeding profusely from either the groin or lower abdomen.

One of our chiefs said, "Danny, go over there by Bobby Lozraites. We have another shooting victim there."

I went over to where Bobby was. He was by himself kneeling next to a woman of about twenty years old. The girl had some buckshot wounds about her face, left shoulder, and left chest. The man in the street had been more seriously wounded. This woman was in hysteria and in a lot of pain.

"Just keep talking to her, Danny," Bobby told me.

I got her attention and reassured her that she was going to be all right. The Floral Park ambulance was on its way for the critically wounded man, and mutual aid from Stewart Manor was coming for the girl. I heard their sirens getting closer, and then, around the corner came the Stewart Manor ambulance. While they were wheeling the young women to their ambulance, her mother showed up, hysterical.

"That's my daughter," she gasped.

I put my arm around her and reassured her that her daughter was in stable condition. Police Officer Dennis Nicholson was nearby and walked over to us.

"Your daughter is being taken to Nassau Hospital," he told her. "I'm very busy right now and must move on, but I know your daughter is all right."

After she left, I was standing with Chief Kenny Lynch and Bobby Lozraites. We saw a car moving kind of fast through the scene, heard a backfire, and thought it was a gunshot. The three of us fell to the ground in a split second. Police Officers Nicholson and Crisalli stopped the car and told the occupants to get out. We stood up once we found out it was safe.

Thinking these guys were suspects in the shooting, I told Chief Lynch, "The cops should just shoot these bastards."

He shook his head. "I agree with you."

Paul Abbruzzese showed up at this point. "What the hell happened here?" he asked. He told me to get the yellow tape from the truck. We had to use the yellow tape to seal off the scene from onlookers, so that the Nassau Police Crime Scene Unit could come to investigate. There was a lot of blood and a pile of vomit where the man was lying.

On the way home, I turned on my radio and heard the Air Supply song, "All Out of Love." That song reminded me of this incident every time I heard it thereafter. When I got home, it was dinnertime and I was pretty upset. I sat down at the table and forced myself to eat. My mother was upset to see me so distraught.

When my father came into the dining room, he tried to reassure me. "Well, you tried to save the person. You did all you could, and you're not the one who did the shooting." He was right. It was just going to take a little time for me to get over this. I had a half of a shot of brandy to calm me down. After dinner, I drove back to the firehouse.

By the time I got there, the ambulance had already returned from the hospital. A cop was sitting in his patrol car on the ramp, and I heard over his radio that the man was in surgery and was listed as critical. Gilbert Luger, an EMT from the Active Engine Company, was there. His pants were covered with blood. He had been on the ambulance when they'd taken the man who was shot to the hospital.

"I better go home and change before I start smelling like this guy," he said.

Garry, who was also on the ambulance, said, "It usually doesn't get that messy. Only one time I saw more blood than that, and it was when that kid stabbed himself in the throat."

The most reliable information that I got about the incident was that there had been a love triangle among the woman who was shot, the man who was shot, and a resident of the nearby apartment complex. The man who was shot had been banging on the door of the apartment, and the woman had been with him. His friends were the ones who had been in the car that had backfired at the scene. They were egging him on to fight with the resident. Meanwhile, the resident took a shotgun and shot through the door. The shot hit the man in the femoral artery and the buckshot hit the woman. The man ran out to the street, bleeding profusely. When he got to the street, he collapsed. Gilbert Luger, who was nearby, ran over to the critically wounded man and saw a wound that he later described looking like "someone had taken an ice cream scoop and gouged a chunk of meat out of his leg." The only thing that Gill could do at that point was stick his fist in the wound to stop the bleeding.

Shortly after, Garry Gronert showed up. He first assisted Gill and then asked a cop, "Are we in danger of being shot?" The cop told him that the shooter was presently being questioned. Therefore, he and Gill continued providing life support until the patient was put into the ambulance. Gill had his fist in the wound all the way to the hospital. He was later given an award for his heroism and for saving the man's life.

At the firehouse one of the Dempsey twins said, "This guy is going to make it. I know him. He was close to death so many times."

As Dempsey predicted, the man did, in fact, walk out of the hospital.

Gill later described the experience as, "Fun—the whole thing."

After I heard the story, I learned that you couldn't take the law into your own hands. The guys that Chief Lynch and I had thought were the shooters had not, in fact, been the shooters.

In the middle of August, I went to the Hamptons of Long Island with my parents. It was time for me to get away for a while. My average for the fire department was so high that I didn't even put in an excuse form. We were only going to be gone for a few days anyway.

It was my birthday and we planned to go out for dinner after Saturday Evening Mass at St. Rosalie's Church in the Hamptons. At that time, I was not a real big seafood lover. I always stayed away from shellfish. But, for some reason, that night I had a longing for a steamed lobster. I think it was the smell of the ocean that gave me the craving. I had never had lobster before. After the mass was over, we went to the Chart Inn restaurant. It was there that I had my first lobster. I learned that I really like lobster. It was really good.

Afterward, my parents went to the motel, and I went and hung out at a tavern down the street. I got talking to a woman and her young niece. After awhile, I went to the motel, where we watched the news and saw the funeral of a New York City battalion chief who had died in the line of duty. That was a bad year for the FDNY. In March of that year, my father had heard about a fireman who'd been killed in East New York. My father had had a gut feeling that he would know the fireman once they released his name. He took me out to eat at Peter Luger's in Great Neck, and on the way home, we listened to the news. They said that the fireman killed was Lieutenant Robert Dolney.

My father buried his forehead in one hand, still driving with the other. "Do you know who that was?"

"Isn't he the one I was playing horseshoes with at the picnic?" I said.

"Yes, that was him," he said. "Boy, is this a kick in the ass."

It turned out that a building had collapsed on the firefighter while he was throwing two probationary firemen out of the way of falling debris.

In June of that year, another firefighter was killed when he tried to rescue a probationary fireman on a rope. While they were sliding down the rope, the rope snapped and they both fell to their deaths. The veteran fireman was Larry Fitzpatrick and the probationary fireman was Gerard Frisbe. My father had worked with Fitzpatrick's father who was also a fireman in the FDNY.

Now, on this small vacation with my parents, the third fireman killed that year was being laid to rest—the chief whose funeral was on the news.

Fall of 1980

SEPTEMBER ROLLED AROUND AND SCHOOL began again. I had three more courses to take before I was finally able to graduate. I had originally planned to graduate in June of 1980 but had needed nine more credits, so I had to wait until the end of the fall semester of that year.

Shortly before classes started, I started a part-time job at Koenig's Restaurant as a busboy. When classes started, I kept a policy of responding to daytime calls only if the message came over at least one hour before I was to get up for classes. So, if I had to get up at 8:00 that morning, I would only go to calls that came in no later than seven, since rescue calls usually took about one hour.

I was able to respond to one such call, since it wasn't going to interfere with me getting to school on time. I responded in the ambulance to the location on Jericho Turnpike, near the Reliance firehouse. It was a man in a car having an apparent insulin-shock episode. Chuck Zuba, from the Reliance Engine Company was trying to give the patient orange juice. The patient's pupils were as small as pinpoints and his face was pouring sweat. He was crying in a way that might give the impression that he was having a psychotic paranoid episode. If he'd been a teenager, you would have sworn it was a reaction to a hallucinogenic drug. I pulled the trundle close to the car.

"Try to relax," I told him.

"This in involuntary, Dan," Chuck told me. "He's going to come out of this when we get him in the bus."

We placed the patient in the bus and took off to the hospital.

I asked, "Did you take your insulin today?"

In a shaky voice, he said, "Yes, I think I'm coming to   I think I'm coming to." He then took a deep breath and started to laugh. From that point on, he seemed in a more normal state of mind. "I had breakfast and I did take my insulin." He looked at the patch on my jacket and said, "Boy, I've heard a lot of good things about you guys from Rescue."

On the way home from the hospital, Chuck told me that he'd known what had been wrong with the guy because he'd dealt with the same situation with his father, who was also diabetic. "I remember my father, God rest his soul. When he would come home from a fire and be in a shock, I would make him eat an orange, and he would come right out."

As we dropped Chuck off at the Reliance firehouse, Paul Abbruzzese yelled out to him, "Good job, Chuck!"

A common mistake that people make with diabetics is to assume they are drunk or on drugs. In a diabetic coma, there is too much sugar in the blood and the patient has the smell of acetone on his or her breath—a smell that resembles alcohol. With insulin shock, which was the case with this patient, there is not enough sugar in the blood, because the insulin the patient took overpowered the sugar. This results in a physical reaction that resembles one often associated with drug abuse. The pupils will shrink to pinpoint-size. The patient will sweat and act incoherently.

This man had eaten before taking his insulin, as he was supposed to, but I remember right around the time of that call, we had seen several diabetics with the same problem, and learned there was a new kind of diabetic medication that wasn't agreeing with some patients. I remember having a call for a young man, and the police were trying to tell his parents that he had a drug problem. I did not believe that, because he was too coherent after taking the orange juice. He denied being a diabetic, yet he said he got relief from the orange juice. I knew he must have low blood sugar, the opposite of diabetes.

A few weeks later, I met his mother. She recognized me as being on the Rescue team during the call for her son. When I asked her how he was doing, she said, "He's fine. It was hypoglycemia." That meant he didn't have enough sugar in his blood and would have to take medication to increase those levels.

On another day during the fall of 1980, I was on my way to school. I heard the sirens go off for a rescue call, but I couldn't respond because I had to get to school. I made a right turn onto Jericho Turnpike and saw some police cars with their lights flashing at the scene of an accident. Since I was passing by, I felt that I had to stop and give assistance. There were two cars involved. One car was on the side of the road with two occupants and the other was in the intersection with one occupant. I went to the car with two occupants first. A man was the driver and his wife was in the passenger seat. The man, however, was out of the car walking around. She was sitting in the car and in a lot of pain. Ex-Chief George Rettinger was holding her hand and reassuring her.

I asked where she was hurt. She told me that her right hip was bothering her. The man was in more emotional distress than in physical pain. I checked his pulse and it was kind of slow. A cop told me to check the occupant in the other car. She was upset. I reassured her that the other people were going to be all right. The ambulance responded, with Bobby Meehan and Pete Feehan as the crew. They used a halligan tool to open the door of the car where the woman was sitting.

I asked Chief Gehring, "Do you think we should call for mutual aid, since the woman in the other car might want to go to the hospital?"

"Yes," he said without hesitation. He pulled his radio from his belt and called Firecom to bang out New Hyde Park for an ambulance.

I heard the ambulance coming down Jericho Turnpike. Once it arrived, I gave all of the information that I had gotten from the patients to Captain Ostipwko. He then released me from the scene, since I had to get to school. This was one of those instances that Marc Krauss had talked about, in which you felt like a guardian angel—responsible to take care of anything that happened around you. That's the way I felt that day. I just had to stop to attend to the situation even though I had classes to get to.

It was October. The days were getting shorter and shorter. By nightfall, we had a call at Doctor Cordero's office for a patient who had stopped breathing. As usual, I raced to the firehouse to make the truck. (The ambulance was still out of service.) I jumped on board, and on the way to the call I set up the resuscitator. When we arrived, I jumped out of the truck. I walked briskly into the doctor's office past the waiting area. We decided that we were not going to waste any time.

Archie Cheng took the young girl in his arms and carried her out to the truck. I must have jumped into the truck, but I don't remember doing so. I just remember putting the resuscitator mask on the girl's face and then forcing one breath every five seconds. She had a pulse, so she did not need any CPR compressions. Doctor Cordero jumped in the truck and stood next to me the whole way to the hospital. The chief complaint, I learned, was an asthmatic attack, and the patient was not getting any air exchange. I had to assist her with her breathing for most of the way to the hospital, and the doctor used our suction unit to suction her airway.

He whispered in my ear. "She is asthmatic and is a little retarded, okay?"

I nodded to indicate I understood the situation.

While I was assisting her with her breathing, she was saying something to me, but I could not make out what. She regained enough consciousness to try to speak, but the bronchi in her lungs were still having spasms. The doctor took a stethoscope and listened for air exchange. He couldn't hear spontaneous air exchange, so he shook his head and told me to continue assisting her. I agreed because she wasn't demanding air from the resuscitator, which meant she wasn't breathing on her own.

As we pulled into Mineola, where the Nassau Hospital was, the patient started to have a convulsion. We just let her convulse and only put our hands on her to protect her from falling. When she stopped convulsing, I noticed that she was breathing on her own. She was sucking air out of the resuscitator.

At the hospital, as we were carrying her out of the truck, she regained full consciousness and asked, "Will I get better?"

They wheeled her into the emergency room, and the doctor stayed at the hospital with her.

I stayed with the truck and cleaned it up for the next run. As the night passed, I learned that the next run would happen sooner than I thought.

I went home. Later on that night, another call came over for a patient who was having difficulty breathing. It seemed like it was going to be a routine call. I went to the firehouse and responded in the heavy-duty rescue truck. The call was not too far away—just a block or two. It was in an apartment complex on Tulip Avenue. I went into the apartment, and there was a woman leaning over a piece of furniture. It might have been a chest of drawers; I don't remember. She was obviously in a lot of distress. Her husband and son were giving us information on her medications and medical history. The woman had a history of emphysema. She did not feel comfortable sitting down, which was a tough situation because we had to carry her to the truck in some fashion. With a case like this, we had to suspect there was fluid in the lungs and therefore could not lay her down. She was on oxygen the whole time. We put her on the stair chair so she would be in a sitting position.

She began to panic. "I can't breathe!" she cried.

While Mike Ostipwko was strapping her in the chair, I put my arm around her and talked to her in an attempt to reassure her. Then, while they were carrying her out, I noticed her eyes rolling and she was losing consciousness. Her son was beginning to panic. I knew there was not a moment to lose, so I went to the back of the truck and turned on the resuscitator. Mike and someone else quickly carried her inside. In less than a minute, they had unstrapped her from the chair and placed her on the trundle. Mike could not feel a pulse. I put the resuscitator mask over her nose and mouth, and saw that she was not breathing. I forced air into her lungs. Meanwhile, Mike began CPR compressions. Jim Friedman hooked her up to the telemetry and there was no rhythm.

Her son looked into the truck from outside, and when he saw us doing CPR, he said, "Oh, God, look. She's not breathing!"

I heard the side door of the truck shut, and looked over and saw her son. He was obviously in a panic. Some of our guys who had stayed back were talking to him and trying to calm him down.

After Mike did a few more CPR compressions, a rhythm came up on the screen. He then stopped the compressions and told me to continue to ventilate her. The rhythm rose to about thirty beats a minute. Her pulse then increased from thirty to forty, and then forty to fifty. I felt confident that her heart was going to keep on beating for us. She regained some of her breathing, but the breaths were agonal respirations, which would not be able to sustain her life. So I continued assisting her with the resuscitator. The driver warned us that he was going to make a sharp turn.

"Could someone brace me so I don't fall?" I asked.

Without hesitation, Jim Friedman held onto the bars on the ceiling of the truck and pushed his body up against mine. We arrived at the hospital a short time later. When we wheeled the woman into the emergency treatment room, the hospital staff began to undress her. She was lying flat.

A doctor came in and said, "If she's got emphysema, you better raise her head."

A nurse raised the head of the hospital bed. Once the hospital staff was taking care of her, we left the treatment room. We handed over the paperwork, got the patient signed in, and then headed back home.

This call was kind of like *déjà vu*—much like the call we'd had about a half a year earlier for the woman named Enrica. Mike Ostipwko had worked on both of them. They'd both had difficulty breathing and brief periods of cardiac arrest. Last but not least, they both had been revived. This woman was released from the hospital after her recovery. In fact, I saw her on Tulip Avenue a few weeks after the call.

When the call was over, I went home and straight to bed, since I had to be in school the next day. It was a night that I could sleep easily, knowing that in this one night, two lives were saved.

That fall, I also clearly remember two calls on the corner of Atlantic and Carnation avenues. One was for a couple of drunken vagrants, and the other was for a motor vehicle accident involving a motorcycle.

The first call was a common-law husband and wife couple who were under the influence of alcohol. The wife was very boisterous. She was rambling out her life story and personal problems. The husband was a little mellower. We couldn't take them to just any local hospital, because of their condition, so we had to take them to detox at the Nassau County Medical Center in East Meadow. The Nassau Police ambulance took the woman, and we took the husband in our ambulance. In the back of the Floral Park Fire Department ambulance were Garry Gronert, Joe Reekie, and me. Garry started an IV on the patient. The patient looked at what Gary was doing while he held his arm out.

When Garry was done administering the IV, the patient said, with slurred speech, "I don't need IV."

He then turned to me with a puzzled look, as if to ask me why he needed an IV in his arm. Then he went to sleep and slept most of the way to the hospital. Every now and then, he would awake and ask, "Where's my lady?"

I would explain that she was in another ambulance and was being taken to the same hospital that we were going to, and he would go back to sleep.

Once, he slumped over, and Joe had to straighten him back out on the trundle. Joe then asked Garry, "What would be his line of fire if he decides to regurgitate?"

Garry pointed to me with an evil grin on his face.

"Gee, thanks a lot," I said.

We got to the hospital without further incident. And then heard a woman screaming outside the emergency room. The doors flung open and there was the wife, being wheeled in.

"Where's my husband?" She cried at the top of her lungs.

One of our guys who had ridden in the police ambulance said, "She was a terror. She urinated all over the trundle, and screamed the whole way to the hospital."

I was glad that I'd been stuck with the husband.

It wasn't long after that we had the second call from the same street corner. I was awakened out of a deep sleep from the radio tones. The call came over as a motor vehicle accident involving a motorcycle at the corner of Carnation and Atlantic. I rushed to the scene in my car. The ambulance and the heavy rescue truck were already there. As I walked over to assist, I saw a man with his pants ripped and his testicles showing. On his testicles was a big incision where the insides were coming out. Luckily, the incision was superficial enough that it did not cut the major artery that ran through that part of the body. They put a traction splint on his right leg since it was apparent that he had a fractured right femur. The female passenger who had been on his motorcycle was also seriously injured.

When one of our men took her blood pressure, it must have been pretty low, because he yelled, "Get me permission to start an IV!"

At that point, I was assigned to help the woman. I observed compound fractures on both her ankles. We put her on the backboard and placed her on the bench in the ambulance. The injured man was placed on the trundle. As we were putting the woman in the ambulance, she lost consciousness.

Father Livoti, our chaplain, said, "Oh no, she's bad." He compassionately reached in the side door of the ambulance and anointed her, muttering a prayer. Since there was limited space in the ambulance, I was reassigned to ride on the truck with the two patients who had been in the other car involved in the accident. These patients were in less serious condition. One had a concussion, however, and was in shock.

After we returned from the hospital, Kevin Tholl and I took the ambulance to go get milk for the coffee. On our way to the A&P grocery store, we saw the crime scene search unit back at the scene. This was not a good sign since the crime scene unit is only called in when at least one of the patients is likely to expire.

This call troubled me for a couple of days, until Paul Abbruzzese, a police dispatcher, told me that the woman had been moved out of intensive care and put into a regular room. It felt good to learn that she was going to be all right.

Show the Kid the Ropes

As I mentioned in the beginning, I met Venard Brooks in the fall of 1978 when I had first joined the fire department. Both of our fathers were New York City firemen and we both were interested in the Rescue Company. His father was a lieutenant in Rescue 2 in Brooklyn. My father was a battalion chief in the Thirty-First Battalion, also in Brooklyn. I could see why Venard was interested in Rescue. He wanted to follow in his father's footsteps. Venard was planning to join the department sometime around April of 1980. By then, he was eighteen and old enough to be a fireman. When the time came, however, he was talked into going into either the Ladder or Engine Company and becoming an EMT so he could still respond to rescue calls. Therefore, he joined the Alert Engine Company. He was loyal to the Engine Company, but deep down he wanted to be in Rescue. He went into Alert in April of 1980, but by the time October of 1980 rolled around, he decided to transfer to our company.

While he was contemplating the transfer, he responded to a call in his car and I responded in the ambulance. He couldn't come with us since he was not an EMT and he didn't belong to Rescue just yet. The call was for a fifteen-year-old girl suffering from an overdose of booze. It was late in the afternoon and most of our members were at work at their regular jobs. Gill Luger from Active Engine rode with me in the back of the bus on the way to the hospital.

The girl was whining a lot and having the dry heaves, which is common for an alcohol overdose. Before our arrival at the scene, she had vomited most of the alcohol out of her stomach, so once in the ambulance, she was bringing very little up. I was holding the emesis basin under her chin while she retched and often had to reposition her on the trundle.

I handed Gill the emesis basin at one point and asked, "Could you hold this for a minute?" He looked at it, wrinkled his face, and shook his head. He then continued with the paperwork. He must have figured that he'd gotten his pat on the back for the shooting back in August and didn't have to do any more dirty work.

Another call in November came when it was still daylight out and most of our men were not home from work yet. It came over as an unconscious female on Jericho Turnpike. By this time, Venard was officially in the Rescue Company. I responded to the firehouse, and saw that it was only Venard and I as the crew. I knew he was trained in CPR and I had showed him some of the equipment on the ambulance before this call had come over. Therefore, he had some idea how to get his feet wet. Neither he nor I were qualified to drive the ambulance; however, since it was a possible cardiac arrest, I took it upon myself to drive the ambulance to the scene and pay the price later. It was a strange feeling, since it was my first time driving an emergency vehicle with the lights and sirens.

Venard sat in the front passenger seat listening to the radio, but he could not hear what the chiefs at the scene were saying. As I drove down Jericho Turnpike, I saw the chiefs and cops jumping up and down, signaling to me where to park the ambulance.

As I parked the bus, Assistant Chief Kenny Fairben said, "Upstairs in the hallway! We have a full arrest!"

Venard ran up ahead of me. I ran up the stairs and observed an elderly woman on the floor. She was not breathing and did not have a pulse.

"Get on her!" Kenny said.

I showed Venard the landmark—the spot on the patient's chest where he needed to place his hand for compressions—and he started in. I took the ambu-bag out of the kit and started the ventilations. Venard and I continued CPR for several minutes, although it seemed like forever. Chief Gehring then called for mutual aid from neighboring New Hyde Park. They also were not responding.

"We'll just stay here until we get a response, if we have to," I told Venard. "As Hank Krauss once said before I was in the department,

'Never lose your cool.' " However, Venard and I were far from panicking, thank God.

Finally, Ed Fry, Assistant Chief Maickels, and Terry Carney showed up. We finally had enough of a crew to transport her in our own ambulance. Venard and I continued with CPR while the crew was positioning the patient on a Reeves stretcher. Once on the stretcher, she was carried downstairs to the trundle. CPR had to be momentarily interrupted. Once we put her on the trundle, CPR resumed. I went into the ambulance and prepared to get on ventilations once she was positioned in the bus. Ed Fry was on the bench preparing to do CPR compressions. Once she was in, Ed and I continued with the CPR. In the back of the bus were Rickie, Terry, Venard, Ed, and me. I remember feeling a pulse while Ed was doing compressions, which meant there was an adequate blood supply getting to the brain. That was what we wanted.

On the way to the hospital, Rickie Maickels shocked her with the defibrillator several times. Each time he got an order to shock, he'd say, "Clear!" which meant for us to get out of the way.

From my kneeling position, I would stand up and away from the trundle, feeling the blood drop from my head down to my toes each time. Then, either Terry or Rickie successfully started an IV line. Finally, with the last defibrillation administered by Rickie Maickels, we got a spontaneous heartbeat. She had an adequate heartbeat, but no respirations. Therefore, I ventilated her artificially for the rest of the trip; CPR compressions were no longer necessary. We left her in the hands of the hospital staff and went back to the station.

I was impressed with the way Venard had handled himself. He had done excellent work on this woman, considering he was not an EMT and it had been his first time doing CPR on a real person.

A few days later, he came up to me on the ramp of the firehouse and said, "Danny, that lady is still alive. We did nice work!"

Kenny Fairben, who was nearby, said, "She's in the intensive care unit and is breathing on her own. So everyone did very nicely."

Later, downstairs in the Rescue room, Ed Fry told Lieutenant Abbruzzese, about Venard and me, "These two guys did a good job on that woman the other night."

"I know," Abbruzzese said. "I heard she's still alive."

I did not hear much more about that woman until sometime in the late 1990s, when Venard and I were talking about the call, and he told me that she had lived for about two years after that call until she passed away.

Later that season, we had a call for a car fire with a person trapped inside. This call required one engine and the heavy rescue truck, along with the ambulance. Venard and I responded on the heavy-duty rescue truck. The location was on Raff Avenue by the sump. Upon our arrival, I observed a car engulfed in flames surrounded by several firemen running around like chickens with their heads chopped off.

When I stepped off the truck, ex-Chief Bobby Meehan was running up to me saying, "Hurry up! We have a badly burned victim over there."

Venard and approached the scene and saw a female who had been severely injured in the accident, although she hadn't suffered any burns. She apparently had a fractured skull and two compound fractures on both legs. She also had an avulsion on her forehead. Mike Ostipwko took a penlight to examine the patient's ears. He observed cerebral spinal fluid, which meant she had a skull fracture. I dressed her avulsed forehead while Venard was splinting her legs. Bandaging her head, I made sure not to make it too tight, or else the bleeding might put pressure on the brain.

This patient was in a lot of pain. While we were working on her, she was squirming around, crying, "Oh, please!" She was also very disoriented.

After we dressed the bandages and put splints on her legs, we used a scoop stretcher to lift her to the trundle. The scoop stretcher was used in case there was any spinal injury; with a head wound of that severity, you could rest assured that there was some form of cervical spinal injury. She was placed in our ambulance and a team of advanced EMTs rode in the back with her. Venard and I were left behind since we were wearing our turnout coats and were needed to assist at the fire scene.

The story I got about what had caused this incident was that the woman had been driving full speed down a side street just off of Raff Avenue, and had hit a tree at full force. She had been incapacitated behind the wheel, and, meanwhile, a fire had erupted under the hood. An alert Lynbrook Long Island man who witnessed the accident acted quickly, parking his car about fifty or sixty feet away from hers and then running over to her car. He did everything he had to do to pull her out. Then, with not a moment to lose, he dragged her to the other side of his car in case her car exploded. Sure enough, the car went up and the whole inside was engulfed in flames. This Lynbrook man was in our village newspaper after receiving a commendation for heroism. Had he not acted so quickly, the woman would have never survived.

December arrived and we were all preparing for the holidays. Venard was no longer the lowest man on the totem pole. We'd since had a new fireman come into the Rescue Company—Joe Oswald's kid brother, Eric. Eric was starting to respond to calls right around that time, so, like I'd done for Venard, I showed Eric around the ambulance and shared some of my knowledge with him. The first memorable call I remember working on, in which all three of us were in the back of the bus, was a rerun of what had happened at the high school the year before, when the kid had overdosed on alcohol. This time, however, the ambulance was out on another call in which Eric and Venard had both been assigned to ride to the hospital with the patient. While they were on their way home from the hospital, a call came over for an overdose of alcohol. The location was at the police station.

John Bennett and I were in the firehouse at the time, doing some kind of work, so we just walked the short distance to the police station. When we walked in, we observed a small but built fourteen-year-old male nodding off into unconsciousness.

John clapped his hands next to the patient's ears. "Wake up!"

The kid opened his eyes.

"What did you take?" John asked.

The kid replied, "Whiskey."

John then walked around, looking for a garbage can. I was next to the patient, taking his pulse. He started to retch, so I stood up quickly and got out of his line of fire just in time. The patient had an episode of partial projectile vomiting.

John walked over with a garbage pail. "Uh oh, too late."

The vomit was all over the patient's arms and shirt and on the floor next to him. John put the kid's head in the garbage can.

The ambulance arrived on the scene about that time, and Eric and Venard walked in. We took some stretcher linen and wrapped it around the teenager to lift him up to the trundle. Since he was a minor, we had to take him to Nassau County Medical Center in East Meadow. Eric, Venard, Garry Gronert, and I were assigned to ride in the back of the ambulance with the patient. Eric and Venard cleaned the vomit off of the patient's arms so that Garry could start an IV. I was holding an emesis basin under the patient's mouth for the duration of the trip to the hospital. The patient had vomited most of the poison out of his system back in the police station and by now was mostly dry heaving or bringing up very little vomit. After Eric and Venard cleaned the patient's arms of all the vomit, Garry started an IV.

When Garry stuck the needle into the patient's arm, the patient started to cry like a kindergarten kid. "Let me die!" he said.

"Well," Garry said, "you can't drink like that. You have to drink milk and get big and strong like us, and then you can drink booze. This IV solution is a strawberry milkshake going into your veins."

The patient then started to hit Venard, but he wasn't too uncontrollable. He couldn't have hurt any of us even if he'd tried, because he was so intoxicated. It was as though Venard were being hit by a limp piece of rubber.

Meanwhile, every time the patient hit Venard, he'd say, "Snowball!" None of us could make out what he was talking about.

In any event, we got him to NCMC and wheeled him into the emergency room. A nurse approached us wearing a white nurse's uniform and one of those old-fashioned nurses' caps on her head.

She tapped the teenage patient on the cheek with her plastic-glove-dressed hands, and said with a southern accent, "By golly, what is this, Jack Daniels? Doggone it, I come from Jack Daniels country and I can't even afford the stuff. Where do these kids get the money to buy such expensive booze?"

When we got back to the firehouse, John Bennett said to me, "You almost got it right in your face. Whenever you get someone whose about to puke, stand behind them and you won't be in their line of fire."

Venard then told us he knew the kid and had once had a problem with him on the street. The problem had taken place the previous winter, when the kid had thrown a snowball at Venard.

"That's why he kept saying 'snowball' to Venard," Eric said.

"You're right," Venard said. "You would make a good detective!

"The funniest thing about it," Venard added, "was when I walked into the police station and saw the idiot with his head in a garbage can. Shit, the garbage can was bigger than he was."

Whenever we talked about this case thereafter, we referred to the patient as the Jack Daniels kid.

Florida in 1981

I spent the Christmas holidays in Michigan with my sister, as usual. Then, for the last time, I came home after the holidays to take my college finals. Once I found out that I passed everything, I went to Florida with my parents. It felt good to know that I would finally graduate from college. Since I was officially out of school, this was also the last time I would go to Florida with my parents.

Since I didn't have to get back to New York for the spring semester, I was able to stay in Florida for four weeks. First, we drove to St. Petersburg Beach and stayed there for three weeks. The place we stayed at was just down the road from where we'd stayed the year before. By this time, I had stopped working at the restaurant, and it felt good to sit down at restaurants as a customer rather than as a worker.

While we were in St. Petersburg, my sister came with her family from the East Coast to spend a few days with us. The previous summer she had mailed me a want ad for paramedics in Florida. I had kind of been thinking about looking into the position at that time, but the thought had faded. On this trip, however, the thought arose again when I noticed that the St. Petersburg fire rescue ambulance seemed to be going virtually all day and all night. I didn't remember noticing that the previous year we'd been there. This time, though, it seemed that every day I heard their sirens and saw them racing down the street.

It was January, and cold for Florida. Temperatures were in the low sixties and high fifties. I wore my winter fire department jacket on a few of the colder days. One night, after nightfall, I decided to go for a walk. When I walked outside, I saw about two or three ambulances from the St. Petersburg Fire Department in front of our resort. It was a car accident. A man was lying in the street being treated by paramedics. He had an apparent head injury. They dressed his head wound and immobilized his spine by placing him on a scoop stretcher. Of course, they also had to put a cervical collar on him to immobilize his neck.

These guys from the SPBFD had their work cut out for them. We volunteers sometimes had an army respond and there was just not enough work for everyone. But in this case, there were just enough men to do the job. I would have offered to help, but my certification was only good in New York, and this team seemed to have enough firefighters and police officers to get the job done. They all seemed cool and unagitated in the face of stress.

I overheard one woman onlooker say, "Boy, they must have to be really trained to do that kind of work."

On another night, I went out for a walk after dark. Across the street from the resort, I observed an elderly man walking unsteadily, apparently with a few drinks in him. Talk about feeling like a guardian angel. I kept a close eye on him, because wherever he was going, I knew he wouldn't make it. Sure enough, he ended up tripping and landing right on his nose. He tried to get back up but was having trouble. An elderly couple, on the same side of the street that I was, was watching the man along with me. The three of us crossed the busy street to offer him assistance. As we got closer, I saw blood dripping from his nose. One of the two good Samaritans pulled out a handkerchief and wiped the blood off of the victim's nose. I went inside a nearby 7-Eleven convenience store and asked if there was a phone I could use to call for medical assistance. The clerk picked up a phone, dialed a seven-digit emergency number, and handed me the receiver. When I got an answer, I gave the nature and location of the situation.

"Okay," the dispatcher said, "Rescue will be there in a few minutes."

I walked out of the store and headed back to the patient. Before I even got close to him, I heard the sirens. I looked back and there was the ambulance driving on the left side of the road since the scene would have been on their left. The couple had been able to sit the man up. Meanwhile, three paramedics came out of the ambulance.

One of them said to the injured man, "I see you banged your nose. How do you feel?"

"I feel fine," the injured man replied. "I'm just looking to get home."

"Do you want to go to the hospital?" the paramedic asked.

The patient said, "No, I'd rather get home."

"Would you like us to take you home?"

"Okay," the patient replied. "I'd sure appreciate it."

The paramedics then walked the patient to the rear of the ambulance, and they thanked the man and woman and me for our assistance.

Before the rear doors on the ambulance were shut, the injured man yelled out, "Thanks very much, people!" Then they pulled away.

The patient had admitted that he was drinking and just lost his balance before he fell. But in a case like this, we had to make sure that he fell because of his inebriation and not as the result of an illness.

After that incident, I replied to the want ad for paramedics by calling Tallahassee to request a packet of information.

We spent three weeks in St. Petersburg, and then we went to Boca Raton to see my sister. By now, I was missing the fire department. I was getting kind of homesick and wanted to get back into the action of going to fires and rescue calls. After spending a week in Boca, we headed back north to home. We had left New York at the end of January, and by now it was well into February. When we finally got home to Floral Park, it felt good. I was ready to get back to work at the fire department.

That winter went by fast, broken up by two vacations. It wasn't long before March came around and then finally spring.

BACK ON THE JOB

AFTER RETURNING FROM FLORIDA, MY biggest concern was finding a real job. The fire department was fun and I liked that kind of work, but it wasn't going to pay the bills. It felt good that I was done with college and I planned to graduate officially in June of that year. As mentioned, the previous summer, my sister from Florida had mailed me my birthday card, and inside it was a want ad for paramedics in certain cities in Florida. I had considered that for a while, but decided to stay in New York since I took some civil service tests. So I applied for a job with a private Ambulance Company in Freeport. All I could do at that point was to wait for them to call me.

While waiting, I just hung around playing fireman. One night we had a call for a house fire on Plainfield Avenue. I routinely set up a first-aid station near the fire scene. The Engine Company put the fire out rather quickly.

Hugo Berta came up to me and said, "Scott up, we're going in."

I was already geared up with my coat and boots. I just had to put on a Scott Pack (Air tank). I quickly put on a Scott bottle and followed Hugo into the house. There was no fire left, but there was a lot of smoke. While the men from the other companies were tearing down the walls to get to any smoldering debris, Hugo and I searched the house for victims. Fortunately, there were none to be found. Everyone who lived at the residence was accounted for. All units were put on a Signal 13, except Rescue and one of the engine companies. We had to stay and wait for the Engine Company to get all of its equipment back on the truck. Rescue was always the last to leave the scene in case one of the men from the other companies got hurt.

Before being released, Eric Oswald came up to me and said, "Danny, we need to go get bagels. I need you to drive since your car is on the scene." Basically, since Eric was a probie, they had given him the job of running for bagels.

I got the okay from the officer in charge of our company and off we went. We didn't care because it took us away from whatever work was left at the fire scene. We drove to Hillside Avenue across the city line to the bagel shop. Then we went back to the firehouse and went to set up in the company room for when the guys came back from the fire.

Meanwhile, Officers Ed White and Bob Heck of the Floral Park Police were at a call to investigate a missing child. While they were at the residence of the missing girl, the girl's grandfather had a heart attack and went into full cardiac arrest.

Back at the firehouse, Eric was in the men's room washing up, while I was in the company room. I heard the police come over the radio, saying there was a cardiac arrest and requesting Rescue.

"Oswald, come on!" I yelled. "We're going bye-bye!"

He ran out of the bathroom. "What do we have?"

"A cardiac arrest," I said as we made our way out to my car.

It was on the south side of Jericho Turnpike near St. Hedwigs Church. We raced to the scene. The ambulance was already there. I walked into the house, through the living room and into the kitchen. There was the grandfather on the floor, unconscious and not breathing. Ed White was feverishly performing CPR, trying to bring him back. Ed's hair was disheveled due to the stress of the moment. Terry Carney put a gastric tube in the patient and then told me to take over ventilations while Ed was doing compressions.

The other family members who were there were in quite a panic. The patient's daughter was crying on the phone, "My father's having a heart attack and my daughter is missing and I don't know what to do!"

We tuned out the excitement and continued with the life-saving efforts. We put the patient on the Reeves stretcher, carried him out of the house on the trundle, and wheeled him to the ambulance. I jumped into the back of the ambulance and prepared to start CPR compressions.

"Are you staying?" I asked Eric.

"Yes," he said, "do you want me to take your car back to the firehouse?" I tossed him my keys before they had the patient placed in the ambulance.

Once the patient was inside the ambulance, I started compressions. At this point, the police on the scene were trying to calm down the patient's daughter.

"You're not helping your mother by getting upset like this!" I heard one of them say. "You have to calm down for her."

I guess they were afraid of something happening to the patient's wife, since she was also in a state of hysteria. If something would have happened to her on the scene, however, it would not have been the first time. I was certainly no longer a stranger to such a situation.

As the rear doors of the ambulance shut, I continued with the compressions. I saw Eric outside looking at what was going on through the window. Terry Carney was the AEMT, communicating with Medical Control. While en route to the hospital, we brought the patient from ventricular fibrillation up to a very slow Brady Rhythm. Terry was then ordered by Medical Control to push an amp of atropine through the IV to speed up the heart.

Then I heard Medical Control say, "Okay, continue CPR and bring him in. It looks like you have this one." By the time we wheeled the patient into the emergency room, he had a full heart rhythm and we were just assisting with the respirations.

When we got back to the firehouse, Eric was waiting for me. "How did this guy make out?" he asked.

"We brought him back, but I don't know if he's going to live," I told him.

"How does it feel?"

"What do you mean?"

He said, "Saving the guy's life?"

I didn't know how to answer that, so I just said something like, "It always feels good. You'll see. You'll save someone's life when you least expect it."

It turned out that the missing granddaughter of the patient was found safe; however, a good month later, in the middle of May, we were called back to the same address. Sure enough, it was for the same patient we had saved before. Eric and I rushed into the house. The patient was sitting in a chair at the kitchen table. He was on oxygen and was sweating profusely. I took his blood pressure. I don't remember what the reading was; all I can remember is that it was high. This time, I was ordered to stay back and Eric got to ride to the hospital with the patient.

In turn, I waited for Eric to return to the firehouse to see how the guy made out. Since I had worked on him a month ago, I was hoping his life would last.

When the bus returned, Eric got out and I asked, "How did he make out?"

"He went into cardiac arrest in the ambulance on the way to the hospital." Eric said he did not know whether the patient was still alive, because they had still been working on him in the ER when the Company had left, but he added, "I don't think he's going to make it this time."

The next morning, we were called back to the same address. This time it was for a relative of the patient. The patient was in the backyard, and Rickie Maickels was taking his blood pressure. It was a very sad and gloomy scene; the whole family was in mourning because the man that both Eric and I had worked on had passed away. The patient in the backyard refused medical treatment, which was okay, since his condition was not life-threatening. Likely, he was just suffering the shock of losing a loved one.

On the way home from that call, I thought about how unfair it seemed that a man that I'd worked on and saved died just a month later. I guess the Lord works in mysterious ways, though. Maybe he was supposed to have been saved on that April night so that his granddaughter wouldn't feel that her being missing was responsible for his heart attack and ultimate death.

Rock Bottom

I REMEMBER WHEN I FIRST started in the company. I had been in only a few months, and I was in the company room with another member, who will remain nameless. He was pointing out all of members to me who were alcoholics. Some were dead and others were still alive. He then told me that he was an alcoholic. He had been sober for almost eight years at the time.

He was old enough to be my father, and had kids only a few years younger than I was. In this conversation with him, he told me the facts of life about alcoholics. He told me that it was a disease and that nobody could keep it from happening to him. He also made me wise to the fact that I did not start smoking a pack of cigarettes a day; rather, I started with just one cigarette a day or every other day, but after the habit set in, the intake increased. The point he was trying to get across was that booze was the same way. He had started drinking by having a single drink only once in awhile, and then the disease progressed to chronic alcoholism. His story made me think it was possible that I could become an alcoholic in years to come. After all, he was right: I had started smoking when I was twelve years old with just one cigarette a day, sometimes every other day. But by age twenty, when I entered the company, I was up to at least a pack a day.

He told me, too, that I would see many rescue calls for alcohol-related illnesses. It reminded me of the time I helped take a woman with an alcoholic-related illness to the hospital, and then a few years later, she helped us try to talk a paranoid and intoxicated woman into going to the hospital. The first woman admitted to everyone that she was in the same category as this new patient—she was an alcoholic. The other woman just spit at her and refused medical aid. She also refused to sign the release form. The police decided that she had to be forced to go to the hospital, however, because she was considered a danger to herself. I thanked the first woman for helping us out.

"Yes," she said, "she spit at me, but I forgive her because I am in the same category." When alcoholics stopped drinking, they liked to help other alcoholics with the same problem.

A few similar cases happened in the spring and summer of 1981. In one, I responded to a rescue call at the playground for a man down in the field. Eric Oswald was on the call with me, and we jumped off the ambulance and ran down the field toward the victim. The cop on the scene was administering oxygen to the victim, who was whining that he had pain and pointing to his chest. I smelled alcohol on his breath. I asked Eric if he smelled what I smelled, and he agreed. Eric also was not a stranger to this guy. He'd had him once before for the same issue.

We put the patient in the ambulance and took him to Long Island Jewish Hospital. I remember doing the paperwork, and I reported that there was alcohol on the patient's breath. The nurse at the hospital was a little snippy with us upon seeing that, as Medical Control had not mentioned anything about alcohol on the patient's breath. Maybe they were just mad because they did not know what to do with this guy, since he was a vagrant.

That call took place in April of 1981. I remember that because later on in the month, we had a meeting in which the chiefs were being elected. John Gehrring went out as ex-chief and Richie Jacobs became fourth deputy for the Alert Engine Company. Anyway, we also had a rescue call the night of the elections for a man down in front of John Lewis Childs School. Eric Oswald, Mike Ostipwko, Kenny Fairben, and I rode in Chief Kenny Fairben's car. Kenny was driving us down Tyson Avenue and then made a right turn on Elizabeth Street. On the way to the scene, Eric predicted that it was going to be the same man we'd had at the playground earlier that month. As we pulled up, we saw that he was right. The guy was in an unconscious state, as if he were in the postdictal stage of a seizure. He regained consciousness at the sound of the sirens, however, and then became paranoid and violent. We restrained him so he could not hurt himself and, last but not least, so he could not hurt us.

Meanwhile, the ambulance arrived and the trundle was quickly brought out. We put the patient on the trundle and loaded him into the ambulance. The ambulance was full of manpower, so some of us were going to take Kenny's car back to headquarters. While we were sitting in the car, waiting for our driver, Eric Oswald walked out of the bus pouting like a child who'd just been scolded. Being that he was a new rescue man, I thought that he'd had a disagreement with one of the guys.

"What's the matter, Eric?" I asked.

"This guy's an asshole," he answered. "He just puked on my jacket."

I left Kenny's car and walked over to the ambulance to take a look. The patient had calmed down, but the ambulance was a mess. Vomit was all over the walls, windows, and even ceiling of the bus. It was obvious that the patient had had an episode of projectile vomiting.

Garry then walked out of the ambulance and said, "This guy was puking on my foot and I said to Eric, 'Hey Eric! He just puked on my foot.' "

Eric laughed at me, and I said, "But I was standing on your jacket. You should have seen the look on Eric's face when I told him that."

After the patient was transported to the hospital, I went back to the firehouse and to the meeting upstairs, just in time to learn that John Gehring was going out as chief and that John Billerdello was to take over as the new chief. Since Gehring was from the Alert Engine Company, it was the Alert Company that had to select the fourth assistant chief. Richard Jacobs nominated Jordan Klahn. Jordan stood up and declined the nomination.

"I'm too old for the job," he said. "I am going to nominate a man who deserves the job—Richie Jacobs."

Therefore, the new fourth assistant chief was Richie Jacobs. Kenny Fairben was nominated as third assistant chief. Then the nomination was on the floor for second assistant chief. Nobody answered, because the person who was to nominate Rickie Maickels was still busy at the call we'd just had.

Billerdello banged his hand on the table. "Come on, any nominations for second assistant chief?"

There were only a few of us from Rescue, so I stood up and nominated Rickie Maickels.

After the meeting was over, I heard Kenny Lynch, who had just been made first assistant chief, say to Maickels, "You son-of-a-bitch. If I catch you yelling at that kid again, I'll bust your balls till they fall off. If it wasn't for that kid, you would never be chief."

He was referring to the fact that Rickie Maickels was the typical reformed smoker, always chasing me away whenever I was smoking a cigarette. That night, I was smoking in the company room, and someone told me that Rickie was coming in and would be mad at me for smoking.

But when Rickie walked in, he said, "No, Danny, you can do whatever the hell you want." He was apparently still in a state of shock knowing that he almost wasn't the chief anymore. Kenny Lynch still remembers that night and he rubs it in whenever Maickels is around.

After the meeting, there was a little hell breaking loose over the fact that there were very few Rescue men at the meeting.

I didn't pay much attention to what all the bickering was about, but I remember Mike Ostipwko saying, "We didn't plan on the schmuck puking all over the bus and having to clean up after him!"

Fortunately, the problem was short-lived. Almost a week after the incident there was a foul odor of vomit still lingering in the ambulance. This was even after cleaning everything up with Lysol. Paul Abbruzzese noticed it when he was doing a routine clean-up of the ambulance, making sure everything was stocked and in working order. He thought that this shouldn't be, as we'd had many people vomit in the ambulance and the rescue truck, but none of them had ever left a lingering stink like this guy had made. So Paul looked around, trying to find out where the smell was coming from. He noticed that the smell was stronger in the air-conditioning vent, which was close to the floor. He opened it up and, sure enough, there was a small puddle of dried vomit inside. He cleaned it up, and finally the ambulance smelled normal again.

This was not the last we'd heard of this patient, and Eric Oswald had him quite a few times more than I did. Eric had seen the guy when he wasn't drunk too. Eric worked for the school district as a custodian at the time, and I remember one night, he had to go to the schools to lock the gates at sundown. We went with him, and when we got to the John Lewis Childs School, we met up with this guy. He was sober.

He walked right up to Eric and shook his hand. "Hey, how's it going?" he said.

Rumors had spread that the guy was like a vagrant. His wife had put him out of the house and the only way he felt that he could get any kind of alcohol was to steal a bottle of Listerine from a Jericho Turnpike drug store.

When I saw him that night, I knew that I would see this guy on at least a few more calls. Sure enough, one afternoon, we saw him again, laid out on a bench on Jericho Turnpike. A passerby saw him and called the police, after which Rescue was summoned. We responded in the ambulance and there he was, in an intoxicated and semiconscious state. We put him on the trundle and buckled him up.

Rickie Maickel's wife, Pat, was standing on the sidewalk close by. "You must have had this guy before," she said.

"Yes, this is my third time," I told her, "and I don't know how many times Eric has had him."

"That's a shame," she said sympathetically.

We wheeled him to the ambulance. When we lifted him in, I was on the left side and Eric was on the right, and I thought I heard the patient retching. His face was turned toward Eric.

"Eric, look out," I said, "or else you're going to get it again." He didn't vomit this time, though. He'd just been gurgling.

In the ambulance, we tilted his head slightly back to keep a patent airway. Many people in this condition died because the tongue blocked the airway causing the person to suffocate.

We got him to the hospital in stable condition. The hospital staff was not too happy with us for bringing him. They thought we should have sent him to the Medical Center in East Meadow because it had a psychiatric ward.

There was only one more time that I was going to have to deal with this patient. I was hanging out at the firehouse when I heard on the police scanner that the same guy was down behind a bank on Jericho Turnpike and that Rescue was being notified. I responded to the scene in the ambulance.

As I approached the patient, sure enough, the rumor about the mouthwash was not a rumor after all. He had a half-full bottle of Listerine sticking out of his front pants pocket.

Then the fireman who had earlier admitted to me that he was an alcoholic arrived on the scene. He had a cigarette hanging out of his mouth as he was approaching the patient. The patient looked up at him, grabbed the recovering alcoholic's hand, and cried like a baby.

"You don't have to cry, Tommy," said the fireman.

The patient asked us if anyone had a cigarette. So the fireman took his cigarette out of his mouth after taking a long drag and put it up to the patient's mouth. The guy took a few drags. Then he told us he didn't want to go to the hospital, so we let him sign the release form. He was taken to the police station for public intoxication.

By the time we returned to the firehouse, we had a call to go out to the police station. Sure enough, we had to take the guy to the hospital. This was the last time that I remember having a call for him.

Someone once joked that we should take him to Syosset, and another person said that Syosset Hospital was out of our protocol.

"No, I don't mean the hospital in Syosset," the joker said. "I mean Syosset. All we have to do is dump him in someone's bushes and we will be rid of him once and for all."

Well, we didn't do that, but it was the last time I saw him. The AA member in the company said that the guy had been committed to Pilgrim State Psychiatric Hospital in Suffolk County.

Another case that year was a female with a drug-addiction problem. We were summoned to the north side of town for an overdose and arrived at the scene to find a female in her early thirties suffering from an apparent drug overdose. I don't remember her name. I will just refer to her as Maureen. It was kind of a sad situation. Her parents were obviously upset. We put her on the Reeves stretcher and carried her to the ambulance.

Her mother said, "She was just released from rehab at Nassau County Medical Center (NCMC). They don't treat this as someone with a disease; they treat it like its garbage."

All I can remember from that point on was Rickie Maickels saying, "Stay with us, Maureen. Stay with us."

I don't think I went to the hospital on this call, but I do remember having the same patient on at least one more call—her final one. Her condition was the inevitable end result of drug addiction. The call came over as an unconscious female at the same address. I walked into the house and there was Maureen, holding a telephone up to her ear. Her eyes were wide open but she was not awake. She was clad in blue pants and a blue shirt. Her pulse was absent when I felt her wrist. I checked her carotid artery. There was no pulse. She was rigid, like she had been lying there for a long time. We placed the paddles on her to see if there were any heart rhythms. All we saw was a straight line. It was apparent that she was dead, succumbed to her drug addiction. We were released from the scene by the police.

Around that same time, we were called to another overdose on the north side of town. This was not too far from where Maureen lived. It was a male in his late twenties or early thirties. Eric Oswald, Ed Fry, Frank Wakely Sr., and I were on the call. We walked into the house and observed the patient lying on the floor. He was breathing, but unconscious and unresponsive. The cops had placed oxygen on him prior to our arrival. Still, we couldn't waste any time, because we had no advanced EMTs on the call, which meant none of us had the authority to administer drugs.

We quickly placed him on a Reeves and carried him out. As usual, we placed him in the ambulance. If I remember correctly, Frank was driving, and Ed, Eric, and I were in the back with the patient. The only thing we could do in this case was to keep him on oxygen and monitor his vital signs. I kept vigilant watch over his breathing. The oxygen mask kept clouding up, which indicated the patient was still breathing. Then about halfway to the hospital, the clouding stopped, and I noticed the inside of his mouth turning blue. I hooked up the demand valve resuscitator and placed it over the patient's nose and mouth. I didn't hear him sucking air, which indicated that our patient had stopped breathing. I had to force the oxygen into him by pushing the button on the mask, which would breathe for him. He did have a pulse at that time. Meanwhile, Ed placed an orapharyngeal airway into the patient's mouth while Eric hooked up the EKG. We were only a few blocks away from the hospital when the EKG started to show ventricular fibrillation. Eric immediately started CPR compressions while I ventilated with the resuscitator. By the time Frank was backing the bus up to the doors of the emergency room, Eric got the patient's heart going again. I still had to ventilate, however, since there were still no signs of spontaneous breathing. There, was a crash team waiting for us at the ER. We placed the patient on the hospital bed and let the hospital staff take over.

As we left, Frank placed his arm around Eric, saying, "Nice job, kid."

Later on that night, Paul Abbruzzese said to me, "You and Eric got the Dirt Bag Award today for saving that guy." Paul, who worked as a dispatcher for the police, was referring to the fact that the police knew this patient as a regular drug user.

There was a big problem with drug trafficking on Tulip Avenue. You would not want to walk down that avenue in the night. The drug users and dealers ruled the street. Many times, I responded to overdoses on that avenue behind the stores. On one such call, the patient was lying on the ground, and a cop had observed the situation and called it in. Some of our men were working on the patient while others of us were questioning his friends to find out what kind of junk he put into his system. The group we were talking to was so bad that we just knew we would be called back for one of the other junkies soon. In fact, the one I was talking to was probably going to be the next aided case.

"What kind of dope did your friend take?" I asked him.

He looked up at me with his eyes half shut and didn't answer.

I asked again. "We need to know what your friend took or else he may die."

He kept looking at me with half-shut eyes, until finally, in slowly drawn speech, he said, "Drugs."

"Thanks," I said sarcastically. "I would have never figured that out if you hadn't told me. Now if you don't mind me asking, what kind of drugs did your friend take?"

"Quaaludes and booze," he replied.

I passed the information onto the AMTs who were working on the more critically stricken patient.

The guy I had talked to also had to be transported to the hospital. Several groups of parents had also responded to the scene, so aside from the two who were taken to the hospital, the rest of the group of young users were released to their parents.

As the ambulance left the scene, I walked with Chief Lynch back to his car for a ride back to quarters. While we were walking back to his car, we saw one of the youths staggering home with his parents. His father reached out to help his son keep his balance, so he wouldn't fall.

The son pushed his father away and said, "Get your fucking hands off me!"

How disrespectful could someone get? On top of that, the old man acted like he was intimidated.

"If that was me," I told Lynch, "my father would beat the living shit out of me."

"In my day," Lynch said, "I wouldn't dare go home and tell my father that a cop hit me, because dear old Dad would pick up where the cop left off."

We got into his car, and while he was starting the ignition, he said, "You know, Danny, this is why I like to see these young fellows coming into the fire department. Because it gives them something to do, and they are away from all of this crap."

Not too long after this incident there was an abrupt ending to the drug trafficking on Tulip Avenue. Surprise, surprise, there was a major, well-planned drug bust in which dozens of dealers were arrested. This was done after a long surveillance of what was going on there. So, some of the users we encountered that night may have been undercover cops. After the drug bust, the drug trafficking dropped, I would guess, 90 percent. Since the arrests, I hardly saw any overdoses on that street.

These days, I feel safer walking down the avenue. The park where the arrests took place is now used by senior citizens attending concerts and a more refined group of young people who hang out there now. We finally took the streets back from the undesirables. This was a job well done by the Floral Park Police Department and the Nassau County Narcotics Squad.

COMMITTEES

I WENT INTO THE FIRE department for two reasons. The first reason was because I wanted to get life experience, since I was interested in becoming a cop or entering some kind of law enforcement. The second reason was because I liked to help people. If I could add a possible third reason, it's because I liked excitement. When I put in my application, someone told me that school, job, and family came first and then the fire department. After you are in for a while, however, the fire department came first, school and jobs came second, and family came last. During this time frame, the latter priority list was the one I was following. I liked the fire department so much that finding real work was low on that list.

I came in to fight fires and render first aid, but when I got in, I found out there was more to it than that. There were committees divided into two categories: company committees and department committees. Starting around April of 1981, when the fiscal year began with new officers, the company committee that I was assigned to was the Membership Committee. I had wanted to be a part of the Training Committee, because I liked sharing my knowledge with the newer members; however, it had not worked out that way. The Membership Committee was a good assignment, though, and I don't regret it.

Another company committee that I was assigned to was the Room Committee. I had been assigned that committee in previous years, but this year, I would be in charge of the probies, Venard and Eric. The Room Committee was a pain in the ass to us because everyone felt that they could leave their garbage lying around and have the probies and Danny clean it up. We bitched about it until they got the drift to clean up their own messes. Sometimes they would leave a half-full pot of coffee for us to clean up and it would grow some kind of fungus if none of us were in the room for a couple of days. It was things like that that made the three of us get together and say, "This shit has to stop."

The Membership Committee, which consisted of Garry Gronert and me, was a little more interesting. We were responsible for investigating prospective members for the company. Since the year, as mentioned, started in April, the weather was starting to get warmer by the time we investigated our first prospective member. His name was Thomas Mahler. We went to his house and met his wife and two kids, one who was a baby. We talked about what to expect in the fire department, being that Rescue was the busiest company. Tom admitted he was afraid of becoming sick on a call. Remembering my own experience of watching an overdose victim get his stomach pumped, I told him that it happens to the best of us. Garry and I weren't concerned too much about that, though. We were doing more of a character investigation to size up the candidate's interest in the company. Tom seemed like a very interested candidate, and he was a homeowner with a respectable family.

So one warm night, around July of that year, Tom was sworn into the department. We accepted him without hesitation. The thing I remember most about that night was that we were called out to a cardiac arrest, but Tom couldn't come with us. He still had to wait until he was told by a company officer that he could respond to calls.

The rest of us responded in the ambulance. Upon our arrival, we saw an off-duty nurse doing mouth-to-mouth on the victim. There was vomit all over her face. She had a child with her who also had vomit on her face, indicating that the child was also doing mouth-to-mouth on the victim. When we got into the ambulance, Eric and I were working at the patient's head. I was suctioning the contents out of his throat while Eric was operating the resuscitator.

One of our AMTs said to me, "Watch out!" and pushed me out of his way.

"Relax, damn it!" I yelled back. "That's not helping the matter."

He looked at me and said, "I have to get the airway in him, okay!"

Sometimes when you lose your cool like that, it just makes the situation worse. People don't like being around you in these situations if you have a hot head. At any rate, the AMT was attempting to insert an EGTA tube but failed because the patient reacted with a gag reflex. So, we just had to suction him while en route to the hospital.

The complication had caused the other guy to get excited, because it was something out of our control. We were trying to save the person, and it was very unlikely that he was going to live. I had learned from the old-timers, however, to remember that it was not I or anyone else who put the patient into cardiac arrest; I was just trying to save the person. In most cases of cardiac arrest, the person expired anyway. That is why I made it my business to compose myself in these situations.

On a happier note, I also served on the Fire Prevention Committee that was chaired by ex-Captain Noel Beebe. During the summer, we held meetings to plan for Fire Prevention Week in October. As the secretary, my job was to jot down the minutes. The important things we were planning for this year's event were an art contest for grammar school students, school fire drills on the Friday of Fire Prevention Week, and a pancake breakfast and art show—featuring the children's artwork on fire prevention—on Sunday. My job was to go to the schools and collect the artwork for Sunday.

When Sunday came, we were blessed with a nice, mild, sunny day. A lot of kids were lined up for the pancake breakfast, and there was a little girl standing by the door. She asked me for a quarter to get in, since she was twenty-five cents short.

"Come here," I said and pulled out the full amount and paid for her. "Put your money away. I'll take care of you." She thanked me, ran upstairs with a happy face, and mingled with her friends.

For the rest of the day, I stayed by the rescue truck showing and demonstrating how to use the equipment. The kids ate the stuff up. At one point, a woman came up to me and thanked me for handling a call we'd had on her son. She recognized me as one of the men who'd been in the back of the ambulance. I remembered who she was. That had been a bad call. It had happened during the summer. A car had hit a boy of about ten years old, and he was crying in an unresponsive state. We later learned that the boy had a fractured skull.

John Bennett had seemed particularly upset by that call. While the boy was in and out of consciousness, John patted him on the back, saying, "It's okay, kid, you're in a fire truck."

I asked the woman how her son was. There he was, smiling and full of energy like a normal ten year old. When he saw his mom talking to me, he waved to me. Sometimes this kind of work could be sad; however, when you saw a child who was so badly hurt fully recovered like this boy was, you felt a strong sense of reward.

I can remember a new member, who Garry and I later investigated, saying he felt the same way. His name was Marty Cook.

"This is fun," he'd said, meaning the fire department in general. "I enjoy helping people."

Marty joined the company in the early spring of 1982, which I thought was a very good year for me in the department.

I had liked working with Noel on the Fire Prevention Committee that year. Noel was easy to get along with and there was no nonsense; we just got the job done with success. At this point, however, the Fire Prevention Committee would be over until the following summer. I still worked with Garry on the Membership Committee and, of course, on the Room Committee with Venard and Eric. By now, I was unemployed and had been out of college for a year. But that just gave me extra time on my hands to dedicate to the fire department.

By the Grace of God

ABOUT A YEAR AND A half before I joined the fire department, I met my friend Tim and his friend Jim on a nice spring afternoon in Floral Park. It was Sunday, and Tim had invited me to ride with him to pick up his mother's cousin, Richard, who lived on the other end of town. This was his cousin who was a New York City Transit cop.

Bringing back a childhood memory, I remembered coming home from school when I was in the seventh grade; my mother was standing in the front door. When I approached my house, my mother said that there were gunmen in the area who had robbed a bank in New Hyde Park earlier that day. The Floral Park Police had observed the getaway car on Jericho Turnpike and gave chase into neighboring Bellerose. There were three armed suspects. Two of them were shot and wounded by the cops, but none seriously. One of them got away and the police were afraid that the suspect at large could be holding a hostage in someone's home.

Richard was returning from work as a Transit cop and he walked into Tim's house and made sure everything was all right.

On that spring afternoon in 1977, I met Tim at his house, I had the pleasure of meeting Richard. We picked up Richard at his house, took him to Tim's house to get a piece of furniture, and moved the piece of furniture back to Richard's house. After returning to Richard's house, we went in and listened to some crazy song he played on his phonograph.

Tim came from a religious family, and I could see Richard was the same way. He sent his kids to Catholic school and I saw him in church regularly. About four and a half years from the date I met him, I saw him receiving communion at the early afternoon Mass. The priest was Father Nilsson. It was a damp, chilly October afternoon with no rain, but it was overcast. I went home and my mother was making a mid-afternoon Sunday dinner. While she was doing that, I played chess with my father. Around two in the afternoon my pager went off for a rescue call. It came over as a cardiac. I responded to the firehouse and boarded the ambulance, and we promptly responded to the call. As we turned the corner onto the street where the call was taking place, Assistant Chief Rickie Maickels was running into the house.

I heard one of the other men say, "It looks like we have something." By this, he meant something serious.

As soon as we arrived, I ran into the house with some equipment. Something about the house looked familiar. It was not the address of a previous rescue call. It was Richard's house. I approached the living room, and there was Richard on the floor in full cardiac arrest. Noel Beebe was doing CPR compressions. All I kept thinking was that my friend Tim would soon have a funeral to go to.

Doctor Shivers ran in, opened up his medical bag, and pulled out an airway. He shoved his hand into Richard's mouth to feel for the trachea and slipped the airway in. Meanwhile, a neighbor came into the house. Grief was all over her face. She put her left hand over her mouth, and with her right hand she kept making the sign of the cross while praying over us. Probationary firefighter Tom Mahler brought in the defibrillator.

After Doctor Shivers put in the airway, he told me to breathe into the tube. Assistant Chief Maickels defibrillated once. After the shock, Richard showed signs of agonal respiration. The EKG scope showed he was still in ventricular fibrillation, which meant we had to continue CPR. Doctor Shivers pulled out a long, intracardiac needle of epinephrine. He told us to stop CPR for a moment. He soaked a gauze pad with rubbing alcohol and rubbed it on Richard's chest where he was going to inject a needle. The doctor then plunged the needle into Richard's heart. He pulled back the plunger of the needle to draw blood, to make sure he was in the left ventricle of the heart. Then he injected the medicine into the patient's heart. Maickels tried to defibrillate again. There was still no response. Richard was still clinically dead.

Doctor Shivers then said, "Okay, let's move him."

We continued CPR and placed him on the Reeves stretcher. The grief-stricken neighbor was still blessing us with the sign of the cross as we carried the patient outside to the trundle. Richard's teenage son was crying over a friend's shoulder as he took one last look at his father before we drove him away. The neighbor was still blessing us with tears of sadness in her eyes.

I got into the back of the ambulance and resumed CPR compressions after they wheeled the patient in. Father Nilsson anointed him with the last rites. Doctor Shivers tried one last dose of epinephrine. He told me to stop CPR and then he injected the needle into the patient's heart for the second time. Then he gave me the okay to resume.

It was hard to believe that just about an hour before all of this, I had seen the patient in church receiving communion, and now the same priest was giving this man his last rites.

Finally, we were off to the Nassau Hospital, with a police car escorting us, its sirens wailing. Maickels was given an order from Medical Control to defibrillate. Noel Beebe, who was working ventilations, checked for a pulse. There was none. We let the new guy, Tom Mahler, resume compressions since I was getting tired.

The Floral Park Police escort turned us over to the Garden City Police, as we made the right turn on Stewart Avenue toward Garden City.

Then Tom, sounding out of breath, said, "I'm getting something on the scope."

He stopped CPR and we saw that there was a slow Brady Rhythm showing, of about thirty beats per minute. That rate rapidly increased to a normal Sinus Rhythm, and then Noel Beebe noticed signs of spontaneous respirations.

He looked at the EKG scope and said, "I wish my EKG looked that good."

On the way home from the hospital we were wondering whether Richard would live as a vegetable, in a coma, for the rest of his life, or walk out of the hospital. As much as we had gotten him breathing on his own, he had never regained consciousness while in our hands.

We pulled up to Richard's house to relieve the Rescue members who had driven their cars to the scene, and neighbors had gathered outside. It was like they were waiting patiently for us, to see how he made out. Of course, it did not look too good for him at this point. One of the waiting neighbors, however, was the lady who had been praying over us earlier inside the house. And the others I recognized from our church. I knew a lot of prayers had gone out, and were going out, to their stricken neighbor.

A week or two went by, and Tim's sister delivered the local newspaper to my house and told my mother that Richard was doing well. She reported that he was sitting up, talking to people. Then, when Tim came home for the Christmas and Easter holidays that year, he kept telling everyone that I had saved his cousin, as if I had done it all alone. I'm not one to take all of the credit, so I made it clear that it was a team effort by all of the Rescue guys who worked on him, and, of course, by Doctor Shivers, who was also a good friend of Tim's family.

The following summer was the first time I saw Richard up and walking around. We were called to a house on his block for a problem with a five- or six-month-old baby. It turned out that the baby had fallen and cut on her lip. She was not seriously hurt, but just had a lot of blood. Richard was now one of the concerned neighbors, standing and talking among a small crowd of people.

Just about seven years after the call we had on Richard, Tim's aunt passed away. At the funeral home where she was reposing, I saw Richard with his wife.

"Dan, there's my cousin that you saved," Tim told me. "Go up to him and introduce yourself."

"No, I can't do that," I said. "It's too personal."

"Okay, I'll tell him." Tim walked over to him and pointed at me.

Richard and his wife approached me together, and he said, "I'm sorry, I don't remember you that day because I was asleep."

He shook my hand and then he and his wife told me their version of the story: He collapsed and his wife had immediately started CPR, which was a very crucial part in saving his life. As it turned out, there were another two points in his favor. First of all was his age. He was forty-five when it happened—not too old and not too young. They say that the older you are, the more likely you survive a cardiac arrest. The second thing he had going for him was that it happened in the fall when the weather was getting colder. More people survive cardiac arrest in cold weather than in warm weather. If you want to put in a third advantage, it would be the thing that was wrong with his heart at the time of the incident. He described it as a short circuit from the electrical impulse of the heart down to the ventricles, which indicates there was little if any damage to the heart.

About seventeen or eighteen years after the incident, I was sitting at the local Knights of Columbus bar, a Catholic men's organization, when who came up to sit next to me, but Richard himself. He ordered two Cokes and sat chatting with me. By this time, he was long retired from the police department. He talked about his son, who was a detective in the NYPD. I talked about the fire department. I specifically remember talking about how we had just gone house to house to collect donations from people. I told him how much I hated going around begging for money from residents.

"They don't have to come begging to me," he said. "I don't remember what happened that day I had my heart attack, but what I do know is that I was dead and the fire department brought me back to life. So when my doorbell rings and it is a firefighter, that check is ready. They will never leave my house without money."

This all happened about the time I was getting ready to become an inactive member, known as an associate member. I was pushing my twentieth year, which was required for associate membership.

WHEN IT HITS HOME

IN THE FALL OF 1980, I completed my last semester of college, although I didn't officially graduate until June of 1981. After finals were over, as mentioned, I took that four-week vacation in Florida with my parents. This was the last vacation I would take with them. At that point, I would be on my own.

It was clear when I came home from vacation that it was time to start looking for full-time work, and, again, as mentioned, I put in an application for an organization that held three private ambulance companies. This was in addition to the packet of information I had sent away for while in Florida, in response to the want ad regarding paramedic work.

Soon after, I was sitting in Arp's Bar next to the firehouse, and in walked Hank Krauss, Marc's father. He told me that Marc might be getting a job with the Village Department of Public Works and that, if so, he would be looking for a replacement for his present job as a messenger. The job sounded attractive, so I went with Marc on a few of his runs to learn more. However, Marc was never contacted for the Village job, so that plan didn't work out for me.

Around March of that year, I had the house to myself when my parents went on a ten-day vacation to Mexico. I would stay home during the day, listening to a new FM country music station, 106.7 FM, responding to routine rescue and fire calls as needed, and watching television. So far, 1981 was starting off as a good year.

By April, my parents were home from Mexico, and I started a full-time job as an EMT for the private ambulance company. My first few days were spent riding in an ambulette, a vehicle to transport people who were able to walk. Most of these patients were going to doctor's offices and not hospitals. It was somewhat enjoyable talking to the patients; however, I was anxious to see what it would be like riding the ambulance.

My first day on the ambulance was a nasty, rainy day, transporting a cancer patient from the hospital to his home. My job was to help people who were waiting to die from either terminal illness or old age. It definitely was not like working for the Rescue Company. The best kind of job was being an EMT in the city ambulance or the Nassau County Police ambulance. There, you dealt with true emergencies. That was the kind of job I was volunteering for in the fire department for no pay.

I was talking about this to a Rockville Centre fireman one day at work. We both liked our volunteer work so much that we were talking about quitting the private ambulance company, as the pay was just a hair above minimum wage and often didn't seem worth it.

One day, I kept the private ambulance at home, since I was on call, and left my car at the private ambulance company. I returned the ambulance the next day. On my way home in my own car, I noticed that neither my left or right blinker was working. I pulled over and went out to find that both my taillights had been shattered.

Partly for that reason, and partly because I was expecting to hear from NYPD about a job as a police officer, I left the private ambulance company around the end of May. I had stopped thinking about the Florida job by now, because New York jobs, in general, paid more. In retrospect, however, that was stupid, because the cost of living in Florida was also much less than that in New York.

The second half of that year, starting in July, was not so great. I did not make the police force, and Marc had not made the Village job, so I remained unemployed for a while. So that summer, I took a test to qualify me to become a post office clerk-carrier.

Also that summer, Marc and his father bought a fishing boat. They bought it second-hand, and it needed a lot of work. It was in a dry dock in Freeport. I went with Marc to meet his father there and helped them do some painting on the boat.

Not long after, in late August, was the Firemen's Convention in upstate New York. How lives can change from one day to the next is unbelievable. Marc went to the convention over the weekend and I stayed home in Floral Park. On that Sunday morning during the convention, my radio sounded a rescue call at Marc's address. I responded with the ambulance and took the trundle into the house. Hank, Marc's father, was sitting in a chair in a weakened condition, but was conscious and breathing. We carried him out into the ambulance and set up an EKG, and Jim Friedman set up an IV line. We put him on oxygen, since his lips and the area around his mouth were blue. I didn't like the way he looked at all. I'd seen cardiac arrest patients with better color that that.

While Friedman was attempting the IV, Hank glanced out the window and said, "Hi, Ed."

I looked up and saw that he was talking to Ed Fry.

"Feel better, Hank," Ed said.

We then took off to Nassau Hospital, where we wheeled him into an emergency treatment room. Before I left the room, Hank called my name.

I looked at him, and he said, "Danny, talk to my wife."

I nodded and promised I would. Those words would ring in my ears for weeks to come.

Back in Floral Park, I went to church and prayed hard for Hank. Then after Mass was over, I drove straight to the hospital to meet his wife Gloria in the emergency waiting room. Straight away, I asked how he was doing.

"He's in pretty bad shape," she said. "He went into cardiac arrest and they are working on him now."

I sat and talked with her. She said that she had gone in to see him before he'd gone into arrest and that he had seemed fine. The only peculiar thing about him was that he was blue around the lips. Both cardiac arrest and the blueness around the lips were not good signs at all.

While she was talking to me, a doctor called her name. She stopped mid-sentence, stood up, and walked over to him. They talked softly for a few minutes, which seemed like hours, as I was waiting to hear the outcome. Then, finally, she slowly walked back to me and, in a calm, soft voice, said simply, "He died."

My worst nightmare had come true. The blue around his lips and the face had indicated a pulmonary embolism. I offered to drive her home and told her she could leave her car at the hospital. She calmly refused. Then after many more attempts to convince her to ride home with me, I finally relented and drove back alone to Floral Park. I went straight to see Father Dodson, a chaplain, and told him the bad news. I felt kind of helpless; I did not know what to do.

"There is nothing you can do," Father Dodson told me in a compassionate voice.

After leaving Father Dodson, I went home and ate the early Sunday dinner with difficulty. I told my parents the bad news, and they advised me to go to Marc's house and stay with his mother until her company arrived, so she wouldn't be alone. I agreed. After dinner, I drove to the house, and Gloria was arriving at just about the same time. I stayed with her while she made a few phone calls. Then, when a good friend of hers arrived, I left.

"Talk to my wife" were the last words Hank ever spoke to me. It was only right that I respect his last wish.

I went to the firehouse and read the announcement of Hank's passing on the blackboard. Then I took it upon myself to erase it, so that Marc would not return from the convention and see it, and be surprised. Little did I know that Marc had already been informed of the bad news.

The next day, I was helping my father clean the backyard. To my surprise, Marc showed up and thanked me profusely for helping his mother during such a hard time. My father offered his condolences as well. Marc said his aunt from upstate New York was at the house with his mother, which gave Marc a break. So Marc and I went to see some of his friends who lived out of town to inform them of the bad news and to notify them about the funeral arrangements.

After the funeral, Marc quickly got back into the swing of things at the fire department. After all, even when these things happen, life must go on.

Summer slowly turned into fall, which was about the time I was working for the Fire Prevention Committee, as mentioned earlier. It was time for me to renew my EMT certification since it was due to expire in March 1982. I enrolled in a refresher course with Danny Bennett, John Bennett's brother. He lived in Melverne at the time, so I drove to his house and we carpooled to Freeport where the course was. It was around this same time that Danny had told me that his father had been diagnosed with cancer and that things did not look good for him. Despite that fact, we both passed the course and had our EMT certifications renewed.

Then the fall turned into winter. Around Christmastime my father pushed me to apply for another private ambulance job in Brooklyn. So I did, and was able to start the next day. It was the same thing as the other private company I'd worked for. I was taking care of sick people who were waiting to die, while I liked dealing more with true emergencies such as heart attacks and even fires for that matter. It was still a job, however.

I worked for the company for about a week before I did my first overnight shift from five at night until seven the next morning, which livened things up. With the previous ambulance company, I had covered the Rockaways in Queens. This company was in Brooklyn, and since I was working a midnight, it was more interesting. We were called to a possible stroke. My partner and I routinely packaged the patient on a stretcher and transported her to Brookdale Hospital. The streets were deserted in those wee hours of the morning. After transferring the patient over to the hospital staff, we sat in the ambulance and hung out for a while.

Soon, we heard police sirens. First I saw the flashing lights and then up pulled an NYPD police car with two cops in the front and two firemen in the back giving first aid to a patient. I assumed that they had pulled the patient out of a fire and could not wait for an ambulance. My partner and I jumped out of our ambulance to offer assistance, but these guys were too quick. They were already carrying the unconscious man into the ER.

A fire truck pulled up to pick up the firemen, and the driver told us that the firefighters, who were just returning from a fire call, and the cops had spotted the man down on the street. They thought that he had been either shot or stabbed and didn't think he was going to live. We never got the prognosis of their patient.

As it got later, the calls started to slow down, so we just hung out at the hospital. When we were called to return, we went back to the bay. I was ready to go home as soon the morning shift crew began filtering in for work. And then someone pointed out my car to me. I looked out at it to see every window broken. It seemed someone had taken a baseball bat and smashed all my windows. I went straight to the Silxty-Ninth Precinct and made a police report. Then I returned to work to call my father to pick me up.

While I was outside waiting for my father, Marc drove by. He was still working as a messenger and had a stop in that area.

"Did some dirt bag smash your car up?" he asked in an outrage. He offered me a ride home, but I declined since my father was coming.

When my father arrived, we rode around looking for an auto glass-repair shop. I was talking about working that night, since they were expecting me to work another midnight shift, and my father said, "No! You're finished. *That's* the job you want." And with that, he pointed to a city ambulance passing by.

We could not find any auto glass shop in the area, so I drove my car home, with my father leading the way. Once in Floral Park, I passed some police activity.

Sergeant Wagner stopped me and asked, "What happened?"

I told him it happened in Brooklyn and he let me go. In any event, my father found out that his coworker's son worked in an auto glass shop in Brooklyn, so I only had to drive my damaged car all the way back to where it had happened to get repairs. I did not return to work and so was, again, temporarily unemployed.

When February rolled around, my parents went to Florida for about four weeks. I wasn't invited this time, because once I graduated college, I was on my own; my father wasn't going to pay my way for any more vacations. So, I had the house to myself.

One night, when I was supposed to go out with Marc, I got a phone call from him. He sounded devastated and told me that he had just had an accident with his car. He'd rear-ended someone stopped at a red light. Fortunately, nobody was injured. There was only front-end damage to his car. He told me that he was feeling down and just did not want to come out that night so I stayed home and watched television.

For the next two weeks, he needed me to drive him to work while his car was in the shop. In our time together in the car, we talked about our interest in the upcoming tests for New York City firefighter and New York State court officer. When his car was fixed, we both enrolled in a class that would prepare us for the written firefighter test. Then, once that class was over, Marc handed me an application for the court officer test. I purchased a study book for each test and began reading.

It was February and the firefighter test was to be given on September 11, 1982. The court officer test was to be given in May of 1982. It was around May 29th when I took the court officer test.

That spring, when I was not studying, I was out with Marc or my friend Tim, who was home for Easter recess. Whenever I was out with Tim, he would brag about me saving his cousin's life the previous fall. He would praise the Floral Park police and fire departments and talk about how Floral Park was just a wonderful place to live.

The first weekend in May, two other friends, Joe and Bill, and I had taken a ride up to Courtland New York to visit Tim at his college. He was to graduate at the end of that semester, so it would be my last chance to see him there. He had been after me to take this trip since he was a freshman.

As May was coming to a close, I applied for part-time work as a security aide for the local high school district. My first day of work as a security aide was the night after I took the written test for court officer. Then, as luck would have it, on my first night, I discovered that the security aide I was relieving was a Nassau County court officer. He told me that it was a good job if I could get it.

The security job was just right for me at the time. I was assigned to work the midnight shift, the pay was around what it had been at my previous jobs with the ambulance companies, and it was closer to home. I remember the first shift I worked as a security aide was a very rainy night.

At the end of February, I picked my parents up at the airport up their return from Florida. On the ride home, my mother told me that my father had had an angina attack a few days before. This didn't sound good. My mother had had stable angina for years, and had a few attacks each year, but was stable. The last time my father had had to take a nitroglycerine pill was in 1974. This was 1982. He'd had a heart attack at a fire in 1971, and later the same year my mother had a mild heart attack. My father's heart attack had been more serious than hers, but upon his recovery, he remained more agile than my mother. He wouldn't become breathless as fast as she would. I remembered that in the spring, when the grass was starting to grow, I had found my father in the house after he'd mown only half of the backyard lawn. I knew that he'd had another angina attack; it was not like him to leave a job like that half done. He admitted to having an attack but denied that it was serious.

In June of that year, I enrolled in an advanced EMT course. We learned that when someone had unstable angina, it was just a matter of time before that person had a full-fledged heart attack. Unstable angina was when someone had an attack at rest, but, so far, my father had only had attacks after doing something strenuous.

In August, I had my twenty-fourth birthday. My parents and I went to church in the Hamptons and met Father Livoti at his new parish. After that, we went to Montauk and had dinner. My father felt well that day. He even said that his heart felt good. A few weeks later, however, when we went to the same place in Montauk for dinner, he didn't feel as well. On the way home, driving on the Long Island

Expressway, he pulled onto the shoulder and asked me to drive the rest of the way home. When he got into the passenger seat, he took out his bottle of nitroglycerine and took a pill. That wasn't good, because he had been at rest at the time.

A few months earlier, John and Danny Bennett's father had died of cancer. Before he died, John had explained his father's situation to us at a meeting and given us instructions in case we had a call on him. Likewise, I was prepared to tell the guys about my father's situation since I was expecting that we might have a call on him.

I started to feel that such an announcement was urgent, however, right after Joe Oswald got married. Both my parents and the Rescue Company were invited to the wedding. I went to the service but not the evening reception, since I had to work at midnight. My parents went to the reception, however, and I was wondering how my father was going to make out. Joe got married on the twenty-sixth of September, and I came home at 7:00 in the morning on Monday, the twenty seventh.

My mother immediately said, "Be quiet, your father is sleeping. He had three angina attacks last night. We were lucky he didn't have an accident while driving home from the wedding."

Monday and Tuesday, he did not eat very well. On one of those days, he had a grilled cheese sandwich and had an angina attack after eating it; on the other day, my mother made him chicken soup. He was in the dining room eating the soup and I was in the living room watching television, when I sensed that something was wrong. I went into the dining room to check up on him. His mouth was half full, and he was struggling to get it down.

"What's wrong?" I said.

He just shook his head, went into the other room, and tried sneaking a nitroglycerine pill, thinking that I wouldn't know. But I knew better.

Wednesday was my parents' thirty-sixth wedding anniversary. I wanted to take them out, but I knew I couldn't on account of my father's condition. All along, he had been seeing the doctor about his problem, and the doctor continued telling him to take the nitroglycerine as needed. Then, as his blood pressure had remained abnormally high all summer long, the doctor changed his medication to lopresso. That hadn't helped too much either.

Still, on Wednesday, he went out and bought my mother flowers for their anniversary. Then he pulled money out of his pocket and said, "Let's get a pizza."

I told him I would pay, since it was their anniversary. After pizza, I went to my AEMT class, which usually went for three hours. This, however, was the longest three hours. I was anxious to get home.

After class, I drove home as fast as I could. As soon as I walked in the door, I asked him how he was doing.

"Oh, great," he said sarcastically, and then told me that he'd had several angina attacks while I was gone. He asked me to drive him to the hospital.

In the stress of the moment, I was afraid that calling Rescue might upset him more, especially since he did not want me to call. I wasn't going to argue with him, so I drove him to Long Island Jewish Hospital. On our way out of the house, he was just standing in the living room with his shoes untied.

"Let me help you," I said.

I bent over, tied both his shoes, and then we walked out to the car. When we arrived in the emergency room, I got a wheelchair, sat him down in it, and then wheeled him inside. I handed him over to a nurse, and she took him right away.

I stayed with my mother in the waiting room for several hours. I was starting to get impatient, and we were talking to a woman who was a little pushy, telling us we should get up and ask what was going on with my father. Even though my mother and I wanted to wait a little longer, the woman got up, walked into the emergency room, and spoke up for us. Less than a minute later, a doctor walked out. He introduced himself as Doctor Heller and told us that my father would have to be transferred to the Long Island Jewish Hospital in Manhasset. In the meantime, my mother and I were permitted to go in the ER and visit my father. We stayed until the ambulance crew arrived to take him to the other hospital, which was not too far away.

Well after midnight, finally reassured that my father was in good hands at the hospital, my mother and I left for home. While pulling out of the parking lot, I stopped the car as we both observed, from a distance, the ambulance crew lifting my father into the back. If I remember correctly, it was about 2:30 in the morning on September 30, 1982, when we finally got home and went to bed.

About 9:00 the next morning, the ringing telephone awakened me. I sprang from my bed and picked up the phone. My mother had already picked up, however, and all I remember was her saying, "Was it a bad heart attack, Doctor?"

The doctor was short and up front. "Yes," he said.

It did not sound good. He gave my mother directions to the hospital and then hung up. I went downstairs and asked my mother what the situation was.

In a shaky voice, she said, "He had a heart attack during the night and he is critical."

We had a quick cup of coffee and made a short stop at the bank to deposit a check. Then we went to the hospital in Manhasset. We asked in the lobby where my father's room was, and the front desk staff directed us to the appropriate floor.

We walked off the elevator, found the entryway that led to the coronary care unit, and located his room. Looking inside, we could not see my father. All we could see was a team of nurses and doctors around his bed—or what we assumed was his bed, although I was not sure at the moment. Finally, a doctor approached us and led us out the door to a waiting area near the nurse's station. He told us that they were doing everything to save his life but that, at that point, it did not look good. It reminded me of when I had sat and talked with Mrs. Krauss, Marc's mother; somehow, I knew that bad news would follow.

Sure enough, the cardiologist came out after awhile, and said to my mother, "Mrs. McVey, we did everything we could to try to save him, but I'm sorry he didn't make it."

"Did he die?" my mother asked in a startled voice.

"Yes, I'm really sorry."

I was willing to drive home, but the nurse saw that I was too upset to drive, so she talked me into calling a neighbor to come pick us up. I called Mr. Oswald, Eric's father. He was shocked to hear the bad news since it had not even been a week ago that my father had been at his older son's wedding. Mr. Oswald came and drove us home.

When we arrived in the driveway, he took my mother by the arm and led us to the side door. Then he whispered to me, "Take care of your mother."

Later on that day, he drove me back to the hospital to pick up my car.

This was the beginning of a long grieving process for my mother, although it didn't show when we were having the wake. It started to show more after the funeral.

Then, to add insult to injury, life dealt me yet another blow. Sometime in January, after the New Year, I was working the midnight shift on my school security job. It was about 5:30 in the morning. I was driving from school to school, and I saw our ambulance on Stewart Avenue, apparently en route to the hospital. The ambulance had pulled over to the side of the road, probably to allow the crew to administer treatment that could not be given in a moving ambulance. I pulled up behind them and was thinking about offering assistance, but it seemed they already had enough personnel in the back. I knew it was a cardiac arrest because I saw Mike Gerbaisi doing CPR.

When the ambulance took off to continue its trip to the hospital, I left and did my last check of the schools. I got off work at 6:30 in the morning and stopped at the firehouse on my way home to see how the patient had made out. I ran into Noel Beebe and told him that I had seen a crew out on a call.

"It was Bob Lozraites," he said.

I was in shock. "They were doing CPR on him," I said. "I saw them on Stewart Avenue when I was at work."

The crew then came back from the hospital and confirmed the bad news.

Bob was an ex-captain that I had grown friendly with. We sometimes would have a few beers together and he would give me pep talks. He was one of guys who had kind of taken me under his wing when I'd started out. I remember standing as honor guard at his wake and seeing the grieving family, thinking that I had been doing the same thing at my father's funeral not too long before.

I remember my mother crying and saying, "My heart goes out to that poor widow, burying her husband on a day like today." It was a very cold and gray winter day in January. At least my father had been buried on a sunny day that was not too cold.

Somewhere around that time in January, we had the captain's dinner honoring John Bennett, who was the company captain. I met his mother there, and we were talking about Bob Lozraites. It turned out that Bob had been getting up for work that morning and had collapsed while shutting off the alarm clock. In turn, I told her about my mother taking my father's passing very hard. She told me to tell my mother to call her, because she belonged to a club for widows and widowers.

The next day, before I got around to telling my mother to call her, the phone rang. Sure enough, it was Mrs. Bennett. They arranged for my mother to go to someone's house for a widow's meeting.

On the night of the meeting, I dropped her off at the house. I felt a little choked up when I saw my mother entering the house and the door shutting behind her.

Later that night when I picked her up, she told me that the organization was the best thing for her. She said she had met a lot of new people.

She was right. The group helped her get out of the house on special occasions and get her mind off of grieving for a while. She would go to a party every now and then and attend meetings. It was good for her to join.

Snow Standby

It was the first February after my father passed away. It was also the first blizzard since he had gone. There must have been at least three feet of snow on the ground, and it was still coming down heavily. John Bennett called me up and asked if I could come to the firehouse for a standby. I accepted and he arranged for Chief Kenny Fairben to come to my house to pick me up, since my car was buried in snow. My mother told me that she would pay someone to shovel the snow the next day and not to worry about it. We knew that this would be an overnight standby, but she thought it would do me well to get out of the house for the night.

When I arrived at the firehouse with Chief Fairben, we set up the rooms for the standby. The newer members had just about finished setting up the bunks for us to sleep on during the night. As I passed the Hook and Ladder room, I saw ex-Chief Harry Whit sitting in a recliner, watching the movie *The Winds of War*, about World War II.

As soon as we were set up, our first call of the night came over. It was at the Floral Park Police station for a male with hypothermia—an expected call on a night like this. We took the truck to transport the patient because it handled better in the snow than the ambulance. The patient was a homeless man stuck out in the cold.

Garry Gronert was driving the truck, and Eric Oswald and I were working on the patient. We cranked up the heat, covered the patient in blankets, and started an IV. After releasing him to Nassau Hospital, we cautiously made our way back to the station. The blizzard was so bad that the front windshield was fogging up. Garry just drove slowly, and occasionally took his handkerchief and wiped the fog off the windshield.

When we got back, we went downstairs to the company room. Everyone was tired and ready to get some sleep—or ready to *try* to get some sleep. Unfortunately, there was a lot of disruption. There were at least two guys throwing things at each other, and then there was talking. At about 5:30 in the morning, I went to the Hook and Ladder room with my bunk. John Florio gave me the okay to do so, since it was his company room. He could not sleep upstairs on the ballroom floor because of the same problem. Finally, we found peace and quiet. Then just as I started to doze off, radio tones went off for a rescue call. It was 6:00 in the morning. Well, I almost got some sleep.

The call came over as a dialysis patient, and we responded in the truck. The snow was still coming down strong. We pulled up to the house, and as I was walking up to the residence, out came the patient all bundled up in a hat and overcoat, holding a suitcase. Usually, we would give someone like this the phone number to the local taxi company and take off. However, this time we took into consideration that there was a heavy snowstorm, and we knew he needed treatment or he would experience kidney failure. So we treated it as an emergency. We transported him to the dialysis center located near Nassau Hospital.

Back at the firehouse, Assistant Chief Bill Green made breakfast for all of the companies. He was frying eggs in a fast, methodical way.

"Boy, you really work fast," one man told him. "How can you do this for over fifty men?"

"I did it in the army," Bill said,

As the day wore on, we had another rescue call for a woman in labor. This call was on Tyson Avenue north of the turnpike. When we arrived, the pregnant woman walked out of the apartment with her husband, and they both got onto the ambulance. I was in the back alone to meet them.

"Is this your first child?" I asked them.

"Yes," the dad said.

I felt relieved, since labor is typically longer for a firstborn, which meant it was unlikely that she would deliver before we get to the hospital. I asked her how long the intervals were between contractions, and she said twenty minutes. That was not too bad, so, again, it was unlikely that she would deliver in the ambulance.

We took off for Long Island Jewish Hospital. We had to travel through a part of Queens County where the streets still had not been plowed. Sure enough, our ambulance got stuck in the snow.

I thought, "Oh shit, she just might deliver on me!"

We called for a helicopter but they could not come out because of the high winds. So we summoned the heavy rescue truck. When it arrived on the scene, we reboarded but had to divert to Nassau Hospital. This truck had better traction in the snow, and the rest of the trip to the hospital went smoothly. Once there, we took the woman past the emergency room, right upstairs to the maternity ward.

It was funny. While we'd been stuck in the snow, it had seemed like forever, and I'd been so worried that I'd have to deliver a baby. But now that it was all over, I was, in one way disappointed that I did not have the chance to deliver the baby, although I was still relieved that she made it to the hospital all right.

By the time we returned to the firehouse, I was so tired from not sleeping the night before. The first thing I did was go upstairs and go to sleep on a bunk. A few hours later, I awoke to the sound of Chief Bill Green setting up tables for lunch. I went downstairs to rest for a while until some of the guys went upstairs to eat. Of course, I went upstairs with them.

There were at least one or two more calls that day, but I can only remember the details of one of them. It was for a possible heart attack. I responded on the bus, and I remember chiefs Richie Jacobs and Ken Fairben at the location with me. A man was having chest pains after shoveling snow, but he was trying to refuse to go to the hospital. Richie and I were uncomfortable about that idea for obvious reasons. Finally, we talked him into going. Richie felt that it was the right decision.

We put him on the bus. I started an IV of D5W, set up the EKG, and communicated with Medical Control. All they wanted me to do was monitor his vital signs and transport him to Nassau Hospital.

After returning to the firehouse, there was a changing of the guard. Members who had not been there the night before were now coming in. Finally, I was able to go home. Eric Oswald drove the ambulance around dropping off several of us. And so the blizzard of February 1983 was all in a night's work.

Unfound for Hours

ONE OF THE BIGGEST NIGHTMARES for an elderly person who lives alone is having a fall, not being able to get up, and not being found by someone else for hours. They could dehydrate, bleed internally, or even die.

It was late afternoon when a call came over for a woman who had experienced such a fall, although all we knew when the call came in was that it was for a woman with a broken hip. I arrived at the scene with Richie, also known as Roscoe. He was a member of Engine One and had just transferred into Rescue around that time. We went into the house, and in the kitchen was a woman screaming in pain. Witnesses said she had been there many hours. I had trouble disbelieving that, because she was dirty and there were feces smeared all over the floor. She was complaining of pain in her hip. We knew we had to move her without delay because she was dehydrated. Also, since we suspected that she had a broken pelvis, she could loose a lot of blood internally without our knowing it. (Because the hip is a highly vascular area of the body, no discoloration will form.)

This was a delicate operation. We had to crouch down in the feces and, using the scoop stretcher, scoop her up without moving her as much as possible. We did it, though, and then put her in the ambulance and successfully transported her to the hospital.

Another similar call, which rudely awakened me out of a dead sleep one sunny spring morning, was for a man screaming for help. It was warm out and the man's windows had been open, allowing someone to hear his screams and call 911. I responded in the ambulance, and when I arrived, Chief Richie Jacobs was coming out of the house calling for the scoop stretcher. I was carrying the trauma kit, so Richie asked me where the scoop stretcher was, since my hands were full.

I pointed. "In that compartment, boss." I knew right away that it was some old person who had fallen. We got such calls routinely, since Floral Park had a lot of elderly people who lived alone.

I went inside the house and was told to go upstairs to the bedroom. I did, not knowing that I was in for a big surprise. There, lying on the bed, was a middle-aged man with a knife stuck dead center in his chest. Archie Cheng was taking a bunch of bulk trauma dressings and placing them on the patient's chest. I looked again and could not believe what I was seeing. There was, in fact, a knife in his chest, but there really was not any blood at all. There was just a little right around where the knife was. The blade was all the way into him, right up to the handle.

As if on a Columbo crime mystery, Archie asked one of the cops on the scene, "Officer, is the murderer still in the house?"

"No," the patient said, "I did this to myself."

In any event, we used the scoop stretcher so that we could minimize how much we moved around either the patient or the knife inside him. We left the knife; one thing about an impaled object is that you don't remove it, as it could be sealing off a severed blood vessel. Archie put the bulk trauma dressings around the knife, however, to stabilize it so that it wouldn't move around while we were transporting the patient.

We took the man to Long Island Jewish Hospital. In the ambulance on the way, we were hoping he would not go into cardiac arrest on us. We would have a big problem trying to do CPR compressions on a patient with a knife plunged into his chest. At the hospital, we put him in the trauma room. All I can remember was a trauma team moving quickly and a doctor saying, "X-ray stat."

On the way home from the hospital, Archie was in a dither.

"Archie, are you okay?" I asked.

He snapped out of his dither and cracked up laughing. "Oh, Danny, I couldn't believe it. There he was with a knife sticking out of his chest!"

During the day we learned that the knife had missed all major blood vessels and, last but not least, his heart. All they did was gently remove the knife, without damaging any major arteries. Talk about miracles.

Another case of someone who had been lying unfound for hours was at the Roy Rogers fast food restaurant on Jericho Turnpike. I responded to the scene in the ambulance. Rickie Maickles was on the chief staff at the time, and he responded in his car. As he lived only about a block away, he was first on the scene. He took vitals while we were en route, so when we got there, we were able to quickly put him on the stretcher, load him into the ambulance, and take off. Rickie and I rode in the back of the bus with the patient.

The patient, who was an employee of the restaurant, seemed too coherent. He remembered counting the money in the cash register sometime after midnight the night before, and then getting hit over the head with a blunt instrument, which knocked him unconscious. He was found the next morning. It seemed funny that someone who had been knocked out for so many hours showed no signs of hysteria or any other kind of emotional upset. Rickie was thinking that he should be having episodes of projectile vomiting, but he wasn't. I was wondering how he could receive such a blow to the head—one that would render him unconscious from shortly after midnight to about 10:00 or 11:00 the next morning—and not have a huge bump. I did feel a slight bump on his head, but it was no bigger than one you'd get in your second grade gym class playing dodge ball.

Later on that day, the police were able to put all of the pieces of the jigsaw puzzle together. It turned out that the patient had self-inflicted the bump on his head to make it look like he had been robbed. Meanwhile, he had stashed the money in his car. In any event, he was arrested for attempted grand larceny.

SELF-DESTRUCTION

EARLY ONE SUMMER MORNING, I was awakened by a call that came over as a possible suicide attempt. I raced to the firehouse to make the ambulance, but it had already taken off, so I drove directly to the scene. I jumped out of my car and approached the call. Garry Gronert was in the ambulance setting up an IV line while the patient was still in the house. He was preparing the bus so that everything would be ready when they wheeled the patient in.

"Danny, go inside," he said. "They need help. Some kid cut his dick."

I thought he said that some kid cut his wrist. Just as I was about to go inside, they were carrying him out of the house. It was a male patient of about sixteen years of age. I went inside the bus as they wheeled him in. I soon caught on that he had not cut his wrist but had cut off the tip of his penis. He looked more embarrassed than depressed; I knew this could not have been a suicide attempt. His pants were down, and he was holding gauze over the stump. There was not really much blood, except for a little around the groin area.

I reassured him that he had not lost a lot of blood and told him he should be all right. He explained that he had been using a knife to cut an apple and had accidentally cut off the tip of his penis. That didn't sound right, but it was not really our job to find out the truth. Our job was to take care of his physical well-being.

When we returned from the hospital, we learned that the police had tracked the blood to the vacuum cleaner. When they opened up the vacuum bag and looked inside, they found the amputated part of his penis.

It turned out that he had not attempted suicide after all. He had been using the vacuum cleaner to masturbate, and the apple-and-knife story was just a fib.

Early one morning, on my way home from work after a midnight shift, I ran into another rescue call involving a suicide attempt. This, however, was an actual suicide attempt. It involved two of our members. One was Eric Oswald and the other was Joe Reekie.

Eric was one with a lot of confidence. He learned very quickly as a probationary firefighter and was mechanically inclined. He was the type of person who could take apart an auto engine and put every piece back together in the proper order.

Joe was also very spiritual, with a heart-wrenching sense of compassion, especially when aiding the elderly. My mother had always referred him as the choirboy.

Eric lived only three houses down and across the street from the scene, and Joe lived only two blocks away. So Eric and Joe arrived at the scene at about the same time. Inside the house, they were told to go to the bathroom, where they found a twelve-year-old-boy hanging from the shower curtain rod. They took him down and immediately began CPR. By the time the ambulance arrived, Joe was on compressions and felt an apex pulse. The patient began breathing but was still unconscious.

I was not there, but since I lived just down the block from Eric, I spotted the action on my way home from work. By the time I stopped, the patient was already in the ambulance. I went to the back of the bus to offer assistance. The young patient was already breathing and had a pulse, but was still unconscious. I didn't know much about what happened until I heard Ricky Maickels tell Medical Control that it was a hanging and that they were en route to the psychiatric emergency room at Nassau County Medical Center in East Meadow. Medical Control, however, advised them to go to the nearest hospital, which was Nassau Hospital.

The patient survived but was severely brain damaged. He eventually came out of the coma and lived with the assistance of a wheelchair.

Not too long after that, we had another suicide attempt. This one involved a Floral Park cop being a two-time hero. It was Officer Jim Ahern. We were having a block party at the Active Engine Company firehouse. The call was just down the street from the block party, so I responded in a private car with a few other firefighters.

Upon going into the garage where the attempted suicide took place, we found Jim Ahern, alone with the patient, giving him oxygen. The patient had rope burns around his neck but was conscious. Our guys put him in the ambulance and took him to the hospital.

Later, we learned that his wife had witnessed him saying he was going to kill himself in the garage, and had immediately called Rescue. That was why Jim, the cop, had gotten to him in time to prevent any damage.

That was not the first time Jim had saved this man. There was another time when this patient was threatening suicide and said he was going to do it on the tracks. I don't remember whether he was going to step in front of a fast-moving train or electrocute himself on the third rail. In any event, the police were called and Jim Ahern was the first cop on the scene. He scaled the fence on the tracks and overpowered the would-be suicide victim, restraining him from any self-destruction until more help arrived.

Because of Jim, this guy was given a third chance at life.

About five or six years later, there was another attempted murder and an actual suicide at the Floral Park Motel. The call came over as a gunshot wound. Upon my arrival, I went into the motel room where there was a lot of commotion. A man was on the bed with a head wound, and a young woman was in the bathroom with a head wound. The man on the bed was in worse condition than the woman. There were enough personnel tending to the man on the bed, so the officer in charge told me to assist with the woman. She was conscious and screaming. I put a neck collar on her since she had been shot in the back of the head, although she was not bleeding as profusely as the man. We put the woman on the scoop stretcher and waited for the trundle carrying the man to be wheeled out of the room. There was blood oozing from behind his right ear, and it looked like some of his brains were dangling from the wound. There was not much blood on the woman at all.

After the ambulances from Floral Park and New Hyde Park had left with them, I heard the rest of the story. It turned out that the woman had been running out of the room when she was shot with a small-caliber handgun by the man on the bed. After shooting her, he then turned the gun on himself. The man later died in the hospital, but the woman survived. The bullet had traveled between her skin and skull and lodged in the temple between the two layers. There was no significant damage and, as far as I know, no fracture to her skull. Despite the emotional trauma inflicted on her, good luck was with her that morning.

Interagency Rivalry

The most embarrassing thing is when two agencies fight at a call. It is very unprofessional and doesn't impress anyone. How bad it looks when an EMT argues with a cop or another EMT over a procedure.

One cold winter night we had a call for a pedestrian struck by a car on Little Neck Parkway and Jamaica Avenue, which is right on the border between Queens and Nassau County. On the scene, a man was lying on the pavement with apparent internal injuries. I was one of several men working on him. We were stabilizing him using the scoop stretcher and were going to put him in the ambulance and stabilize any possible fractures. The New York City Police, the Floral Park Police, and our rescue team were there, but while the patient was still on the cold street, we heard more sirens approaching. Seconds later, a New York City ambulance with two paramedics arrived. I saw a silhouette of one of the paramedics running like blazing glory right toward us. He pushed two of our men out of the way and immediately started criticizing how we were doing things. His partner, who was just as arrogant, did the same thing. He pushed at least one of our men out of the way to get to the patient. Rickie Maickels, who was chief of the department at the time, did not like what he saw.

"Excuse me," he said. He was ignored, so he put his hands on the second paramedic to get his attention.

"Don't touch me or I'll arrest you," the paramedic said.

Both paramedics left the patient to argue with Chief Maickels. They were putting their fingers in Rickie's face and I remember Rickie finally telling the one paramedic to stop.

"The next time you put your finger in my face," he said, "you're going down on your ass."

Well, the paramedic stopped physically putting his finger in Rickie's face, but he kept on arguing.

Meanwhile, our guys put the patient in the ambulance and took off for the hospital. The paramedics and the rest of our men who stayed in town remained at the scene to continue the argument among themselves. They were even getting a little physical to the point that the Floral Park Police were restraining our guys and the NYPD officers were restraining the New York City paramedics.

Bob Stelz, from our company, said that the same thing had happened when he'd been in the Bayside Queens Volunteer Ambulance Company. He was at a call in which two other city ambulances responded, and the two crews of paramedics were fighting over which of them should take the patient to the hospital. In the meantime, the Bayside crew just took the patient in their ambulance, letting the city paramedics continue with their fight.

Not too long after the incident on Little Neck Parkway, I was driving on the Cross Island Parkway in Bellerose Queens, which was part of New York City. I came upon bumper-to-bumper traffic and noticed that, not far in front of me, was the scene of an accident involving an overturned auto. It must have just happened, because I had not been stopped for long. I pulled my car onto the grass bank alongside the road and offered assistance. I heard someone say that 911 had been called and were on their way. As I approached the overturned auto, I saw a girl in her twenties strapped to her seat in an upside-down position.

We freed her, and as she exited the car, all she kept saying was, "Thank God I was wearing my seatbelt."

I heard sirens in the distance coming closer, and then saw an ambulance coming down the exit ramp, going against traffic. It was the only way they could get to the scene because the traffic was backed up on the other side of the road. As the technicians exited the ambulance and approached the scene, I recognized one of them as being one of the paramedics we'd had trouble with at the accident on Little Neck Parkway.

He observed my winter jacket with the FPFD RESCUE patch, and said to me, "You guys are in a lot of trouble."

Here he was at the scene of an accident, and all he seemed to want to do was argue over something that had nothing to do with the crisis going on at the moment. I did not reply, because I did not feel like arguing. I just told him about the patient who had a small bump on her head. He rendered aid to the young woman as he was supposed to.

Now that help was on the scene, I felt it was time for me to go. I went back to my car and started it up. The schmuck approached me and continued telling me that we were in trouble with the Board of Health, because he had made a complaint against us. Meanwhile, back at the scene of the accident, his partner was arguing with a police sergeant about moving the ambulance. A cop then came over and said that I had to move my car.

"Good-bye," I said and took off.

I read in the paper the next day that the first guy's partner was arrested for disorderly conduct, for refusing to move the ambulance out of the way of traffic.

That accident happened in the winter, and the following fall, I became a candidate for an EMT position with New York City Health and Hospitals. I was at its headquarters in Maspeth Queens for processing when I ran into these two paramedics yet again. I was not wearing any marked FPFD attire this time, so I don't think they recognized me. Then, a few of the other EMT candidates and I got talking with them, and they told us they were in the building to answer for a civilian complaint. Why I was not surprised to hear that?

WHAT DO YOU WANT TO BE
WHEN YOU GROW UP?

WHAT DO YOU WANT TO be when you grow up? That was the sarcastic question a lot of people asked me when I worked part time as a high school security aide. Another smart-ass question I got was, When are you going to get a real job? But it wasn't like I hadn't tried. I had taken civil service test after civil service test. In the late seventies and the early eighties, I took several police exams and two firefighter exams. In 1981, I took the clerk and carrier test for the postal service. In May of 1982, I took the court officer test. On September 11, 1982, I took the firefighter test. In December of 1983, I took the physical agility test for the New York City Fire Department. I passed all the tests, but did not score high enough to top the list and, therefore, did not get called for the job.

Finally, after years of agony trying to find gainful employment, in October of 1984, I got called for the New York City Emergency Medical Service. On my first day at the academy, they discovered that my EMT certification was about to expire in January of 1985 and let me go. However, after the appointment to EMS, I had already quit my job at the high school. Fortunately, I had kept my custodian job. And when my previous supervisor at the security job heard that I hadn't succeeded with the EMS position, he pulled some strings to get me back to work in early November of that year.

On my first night back, he asked, "Why didn't you tell me that you were out of work?" "You don't use your head."

I worked for the rest of November, all of December and most of January. In December, I had gotten a Christmas present in the mail: an offer of employment as a carrier for the post office. This was the result of a test I had taken in the summer of 1981. It took three-and-a-half years to get called.

By the end of January of 1985, I went through the whole process of getting hired at the post office. I handed in another letter of resignation at my security job, but still hung onto my custodian job.

The day I was to take my driving test for the post office, I was at home when a call came over for a house fire that was just around the corner from where I lived. I ran to the scene on foot since it was so close. As I approached the house, there was a woman screaming that her boyfriend was inside. She was standing in the doorway leading to the living room. She was very disoriented and under the influence of alcohol; I could smell it on her breath. There was smoke coming out of the doorway. I got down low on my hands and knees and went in. I was crawling around the living room looking for her boyfriend when I came upon two pairs of legs wearing post office uniform pants. I established that they were two mailmen trying to rescue the man. They were being overcome by the smoke because they were standing upright, whereas I was not affected because I was on my hands and knees, and most of the smoke was above me. The men told me that the boyfriend was upstairs.

I crawled up a spiral staircase and into a bedroom. It was kind of dark. The first place I felt was around the bed. I felt a pair of feet dangling off of the foot of the bed, so I held one foot with one hand and, with my other hand, banged on the sole of the foot I was holding.

"Wake up!" I yelled. "There is a fire in the house!"

After he woke up, I walked him out of the room and down the spiral staircase. The man also had the smell of alcohol on his breath. By the time we reached the front door, a crew had arrived at the scene. The woman was being aided by our guys from Rescue. However, she refused further treatment and did not go to the hospital.

After the fire was extinguished, it was discovered that a careless cigarette butt had set a couch ablaze.

About a week or so later, I started working for the post office. I went for one week of training in Flushing and then got assigned to the Floral Park Post Office. On my first day in Floral Park, my old mailman broke me in. They let me walk his route with him. That was a tough job to learn, but like anything else, it gets easier as you get more experience. Little did I know that this new job would put a damper on my fire department average. Like a lot of the guys had told me, when I started working, I would not be around as much.

For six years, I had worked hard for the fire department, but had not worked as hard as I should have to find gainful employment. Yet, whenever I was out delivering mail and heard the sirens go off for a fire or a rescue call, I would feel guilty. I missed so many calls.

I started in the beginning of February, when spring was just around the corner. My first year went pretty fast. I hung onto my custodian job until June. It just got to be too much. Then the summer of 1985 seemed like one big, long heat wave. Boy, it was hot.

In early 1985, just around the time I started at the post office, the morale in the Rescue Company was deteriorating dramatically. In April of 1984, Mike Ostipwko had become fourth assistant chief and Paul Dombrowski had become captain, and some of the guys were just disgruntled over the change in officers. If a patient died, it was Mike and Paul's fault. If a patient was saved, the job had somehow not been done right. The new officers were not treated right at all; I would rather suffer going through my probationary period again than to go through what they went through. Paul Dombrowski was fed up with the crap, so he resigned. Mike stuck it out.

After that, I started to realize that a lot of members were at each other's throats and were just generally not getting along. We had some new members who shot their mouths off without paying their dues. However, we had some good new members too. The good ones were Rosemary Woodcock, Marylou Norman, and her brother Jim Norman. And after them came Scott Baker. I had assumed at the time that Scott was going to be a snob, but I ended up being wrong. A few years later, Scott and these other three new members played an important part in bringing back the morale in and saving the company. Another valuable member was Jim Hickman, who transferred to Rescue from Reliance Engine Company 2.

Getting back to the morons of the company, though, one was the type who would stand around with his hands in his pockets and do little to nothing to help. When calls were over, he would confront me and tell me everything that I did wrong. One night, for example, we had a woman in cardiac arrest. I was in the ambulance on the way to the hospital, working on ventilations. She was vomiting and aspirating. Sure enough, the new member I mentioned was a few feet away, telling me what I was doing wrong.

"Come down here and help," I said, pulling him by the arm.

He knelt next to me to assist in suctioning the patient's airway.

"Get in there," I told him.

He started to gag. Then he turned his head and retched down the side door.

At the hospital, as we took the patient into the emergency room, he ran over to some bushes and vomited again.

On another call I was kind of depressed about losing a man who had gone into cardiac arrest at a karate school, where he'd been taking karate lessons with his eight-year-old son. Here, we had just witnessed an eight-year-old boy lose his father, and this jerk was telling me that this kind of work was not for me. As if he could talk. Anyway, not to my disappointment, he left the company shortly thereafter.

When I started delivering and collecting mail for the post office full time, my time at the fire department was greatly diminished. I would be walking a route and hear call after call on my radio, or hear the sirens blow and know I was missing out. One afternoon, in early September 1985, I was on a route when we finally got a break in that summer heat wave that I previously mentioned. I was on Jericho Turnpike emptying out a mail box, and it suddenly became overcast. It immediately started raining, and less than a minute later, began hailing. The wind started to blow violently. At first, I thought it was just a hurricane; little did I know it was a tornado. The visibility was so bad that I had to wait in the mail truck for the weather to let up.

The rain slowed shortly thereafter, and the sun came out again.

I drove to the next mailbox, and when I got out, there was a big puddle of water with downed power lines all around me. I looked around carefully to make sure no lines were in the water that I had to step in. I somehow managed to empty out the mailbox without getting hurt.

I then heard someone say that a few blocks away, a tree had fallen on a parked car and a woman was trapped inside. I returned to the post office and transferred the mail from my truck onto the truck going to the Jamaica post office, then I clocked out and responded to the scene of the accident. By the time I arrived, they had a ton of help on the scene. Our guys had removed the whole roof of the car. The tree was pretty much just on the car hood. Venard Brooks was in the car next to the woman, who was still trapped, giving her psychological first aid and oxygen. It seemed that the dashboard had collapsed on the woman's legs, pinning her in.

Venard told the woman that the whole thing would have a happy ending, although he was afraid that once they freed the woman, the blood would rush back into her lower extremities and she would bleed to death. Not only would the woman die, but the incident would make a liar out of him.

There were a lot of Village employees and firemen with chainsaws, cutting big branches off of the tree to make it lighter, since it was too heavy to lift off the hood. Finally, they were able to lift it and pull the car backward away from the tree. This was the point when Venard feared the woman might go sour. She didn't, though, and they were able to remove her, put her on the stretcher, and get her into the ambulance. Her vitals remained stable on the way to the hospital.

Later on that night, we were on standby at the firehouse, when we found out that the woman had not only not broken her legs, but had also been released from the hospital with no injuries other than a few minor bruises on her legs.

The next day, the weather was colder. It was fall-like. It was Labor Day weekend and the first time we had felt coolness in the air since the beginning of the summer. I continued my work at the post office, walking routes and delivering parcels. If was funny, though, that before I'd gotten this job, people had been giving me a hard time about not working. But now that I had the job, they were giving me a hard time about my call average going to hell.

After being with the post office for almost a year, I was assigned an auxiliary route for substitute carriers. Each day, I would walk that route, and then give an hour's worth of help to a regular full-time carrier, and that would add up to an eight-hour workday. The auxiliary route covered businesses on Jericho Turnpike and some of its side streets.

I remember a woman who worked in one of these businesses, named Anne. She was a happy camper. She worked with about two or three other woman in an office. She would make the other women happy, too, and they were all just nice to work for.

Every day, I would walk up the stairs to their office and see Anne's eyes looking through the window at me climbing up the stairs. As usual, she and her coworkers would be laughing. I would walk up the stairs and hand the mail to her through the window, and she always had a nice thing to say. Then Anne would always give me letters to mail for her.

It wasn't only them; all of the people on that route were nice. I knew the route really well and I think that made a difference. I always gave everyone the right mail and if I made any mistakes, they were fewer than I'd made on any other routes I'd had.

Sometime in July 1986, I was in the firehouse. Thomas Mahler was the captain of Rescue. He was sitting at the table in the company room and he called me over to have a private conversation. It was his job to tell me that my average was now delinquent. The quarter had ended on June 30, so July was the time when the averages came out. He said that I had plenty of time to get it back up, and since this was my first offense, I just got verbal admonishment. On the second offense, the member got a letter of warning in the mail, and on the third, a letter calling him to council, to answer on charges of neglect of duty. Even if a member had to answer for charges in front of council, the council gave the member the benefit of the doubt, and tried to help him or her.

I was thinking about responding to calls while on my mail route, but Captain Mahler told me not to risk my job, and to just try to make middle-of-the-night calls instead of rolling over to go back to sleep. From that point on, I responded to any call I could without risking my job with the post office.

One such call I remember making was when I was driving my car in town. I heard the horns blow a 22—a rescue call. I went directly to the firehouse since it was on my way home. I responded in the ambulance with Captain Mahler on board. He said he had seen an improvement in my average and told me that I was making a killing. On the way to the call, we heard over the radio that we were responding to a cardiac arrest. Upon our arrival, we went into the private home and came upon a woman in her late forties in cardiac arrest. She looked familiar. I knew I had seen her before. But at that moment, I just couldn't remember where I knew her from. I inserted an EGTA airway and worked on ventilations. She was on the living room floor, and we put her on the trundle and wheeled her out while doing CPR.

The woman's daughter was standing in front of the house, crying and looking me in the eye while I was working on her mother. Then she said, "Gary, is that you?"

I realized that I remembered the girl from high school. At that point, then, it dawned on me that the woman we were trying to save was Anne, the woman who worked at that business on my mail route. The last name of her daughter and the street address where she lived, I recognized from the return address on the letters that I used to mail for her at work. Still, I was hoping against hope that this was not really Anne.

In the ambulance, Captain Mahler was attempting to start an IV on her right arm, while I was attempting to start one on her left. I saw a flash of blood in the needle, which meant I got a vein. I told Captain Mahler that I'd made a hit. He asked me the size of the needle and I said that it was a twenty-gauge. He then ordered me to pull it out because he had hit a vein with an eighteen-gauge needle, which was better to push drugs through. From that point on, I helped do CPR while Captain Mahler pushed the drugs through the IV line and operated the defibrillator.

After arriving at the hospital, we left the patient in the hands of the staff, then went back to the station to clean the ambulance and remake the trundle. Captain Mahler joked about my IV stick.

"Your needle was too small," he said. "You have to start as Post Master General and work my way down to the smaller needle."

Meanwhile, we got word that our patient had passed away.

The next business day, I was delivering mail to the business where Anne worked. Usually, I saw three happy women laughing and joking. This time, there was only two women who looked sad and teary-eyed. I opened the window and gave the mail to one of the women.

"Anne is not going to be with us anymore," she told me.

In October of that year, after the June to September quarter ended, my average was back up to 35 percent. The minimum to be in good standing was 25 percent. This made Captain Mahler happy. Now that I was back in the swing of things, I was able to take a day off and help with the school fire drills for Fire Prevention Week. At one of the grammar schools, we did an evacuation drill, and when the students and teachers were returning to their classrooms, a teacher approached me and thanked me for trying to save her mother. It was Anne's daughter. She told me that she had thought I was this guy named Gary that we knew from high school. When we were in school, a lot of people swore that Gary and I were identical twins.

POSSIBLE SUICIDE ATTEMPT

ONE LATE SPRING AFTERNOON, I was at the bank taking care of business. I heard the horns go off. It was a twenty two. I didn't have my pager on so I ran to my car to go to the firehouse. I heard a police car siren wailing down Plainfield Avenue and made a left onto Floral Parkway. It was Police Officer Jim Ahern racing to the scene. I raced to the firehouse and the Ambulance stopped to pick me up. Hook and Ladder fireman Tom O'Garra told me that we were going to a possible suicide attempt. No information was given about the nature of the incident. All we knew was that we were responding to a cardiac arrest. At this point, we didn't know what we were responding to. It could have been an intentional overdose, gunshot, a self-inflicted stabbing, or what have you. Upon our arrival we came upon a woman in cardiac arrest in the driveway of a private home. There was no blood, so it wasn't the use of a knife or a gun. I just dove into the situation setting up the trundle and helping out doing CPR We put her in the ambulance in the usual way and rushed her to Winthrop Hospital. On the way to the hospital, I was working the ventilations while another firefighter was doing the compressions. Paul Abruzzese was doing the medications and defibrillation. In the midst of all of the confusion I overheard that she suffered carbon monoxide poisoning by turning the car on while in a closed garage. We were unable to get her heart going in the ambulance. After arriving at the hospital, she was pronounced dead before we left to go back home. Paul was talking with her husband outside the ER. I overheard him mention that the detectives are going to have to investigate this incident. They have to do that routinely in a case like this.

On the way home from the hospital, Paul said that while talking with her husband, he found out that she thought she had cancer. She was being treated by her physician for an unknown condition. They were worrying about cancer. However, she was not even diagnosed as of yet. We believed that was her motive to kill herself.

Pedestrian Accident

I was living in an apartment on Jericho Turnpike after being on my own for a brief time. I was loafing around in my apartment when a call came over my pager. It came over as a pedestrian accident with multiple victims at the corner of Plainfield and Tulip avenues. I responded in my car and that was just what I came upon. Help arrived pretty quickly, so I just mixed in with all the confusion, which included much of the congregation of the Our Lady of Victory Church, which had just let out down the street.

Some of the victims were injured seriously but none critically. I was assigned to assist with a young girl in her late teens. She was in mild shock with a possible broken hip. I also noticed a laceration on the white part of one of her eyes. She was otherwise pretty stable. There were ambulances from fire departments from all over, including Elmont, New Hyde Park, Stewart Manor, and of course Floral Park. We took the girl I was working on to Winthrop Hospital. A friend from our past—Paul Dombrowski, who, as mentioned, had resigned from the company—took the ambulance ride with us.

On the way back from the hospital, we tried to talk him into coming back to the station with us. I felt the same way the other guys did. The way he'd helped this young girl had reminded me of the professionalism I'd seen in Paul all those years he'd been with the company. He said that he would like to come back, but had to get back to his regular job.

That particular street corner that we'd gone to was famous for serious vehicle and pedestrian accidents. I found out later that, at this accident, a car had lost control and careened onto the sidewalk, injuring several people who'd been coming out of the church. Another accident on that street corner involved an elderly woman coming out of the same church. She also had been hit by a car and had a serious head injury. Our chaplain, Father Benedict DeAndrea, approached her, anointed her, and said a quick prayer. Venard Brooks and I rode in the ambulance with her to the hospital. She was in a lot of distress and pain. She was vomiting and it was apparent that she had a concussion. All we could do at that point, however, was to administer oxygen. Venard knelt next to her, giving her psychological first aid.

Another bad pedestrian accident at that same corner was a real nightmare for Venard. I did not make it to that call, so I don't know the bitter details. I only know that a young woman was hit by a car and thrown I don't know how many feet. She had massive head trauma that was far worse than the elderly woman's, and perished in the hospital. Now, even after all these years, the family of the woman places flowers on that corner to mark the annual anniversary of the tragedy. When they do, Venard notices it, and talks about the incident like it were only yesterday. It is like he can still see her face fresh in his mind.

DIFFICULTY BREATHING

ON ONE OF MY DAYS off, I was in my apartment doing chores and a call came over for a patient who had difficulty breathing. It was during the day, so manpower was scarce. I raced there in my car. There were only two cops on the scene so far. It was upstairs in a private home, and I could not believe what I walked in to. A huge man, about six and a half feet tall, was on oxygen and in a lot of distress. I had been able to hear the fluid in his lungs all the way down the hallway. I knew the situation was not good because his condition was rapidly deteriorating.

The ambulance arrived about five minutes later, although the wait seemed like five hours. On the bus were Venard Brooks, Bobby Meehan, and two newer members, Kevin Kelleher and Rosemary Woodcock. It was a big relief to see the cavalry arrive. We put the patient on the stair chair and carried him down to the ground floor. From there, we transferred him on the trundle. We made sure his shoulders were elevated, so he would not choke on his own fluids. While we were carrying him out into the ambulance, I observed him slipping in and out of consciousness.

Venard and I were the only AMTs on the scene, and we were both thinking the same thing. We had to get Lasix in him at once, or we were going to lose him. As we put him in the ambulance, I went right to the patient's head. It was apparent that he had just stopped breathing. I quickly started ventilations with the resuscitator. Meanwhile, Kevin and Rosemary hooked him up to the EKG. Venard was very quickly and systematically administering the IV line and getting the Lasix ready. The patient still had a pulse but was not breathing.

Venard contacted Medical Control, and they ordered Lasix. We asked Bobby to pull over. While we were momentarily stopped, Venard pushed the Lasix through the IV line. About a minute later, the patient started breathing again. However, he was still unconscious and in bad shape. As we pulled up to the ER, the staff was waiting for us. I told them to be careful because this was a big, big man. This was one more job well done by Venard.

However, the story did not end there. A few weeks later, we had the same patient with the same problem. There were a bunch of us on the call, because it happened in the evening this time, and we had a lot of manpower that time of day. Venard and I were assigned to ride in the ambulance and, sure enough, Venard got to push another ampule of Lasix to stabilize the patient's breathing. The patient was in the same kind of distress as he had been during the first incident, but did not stop breathing this time. He did not even lose consciousness. After Venard pushed the drugs into the IV line, the patient started to stabilize and his breathing became less labored. When I asked the patient how he was doing, he answered that he felt much better.

Venard had pulled it off again. Unfortunately, a few weeks later, we heard that the patient passed away from further complications with the same condition.

THE FOUR-HUNDRED-POUND OVERDOSE

WE WERE SUMMONED TO AN apartment complex on Tulip Avenue for an overdose. It was in the afternoon and, as usual, manpower was scarce at that time of the day. Bobby Meehan was driving the ambulance, and Ed Rothenberg, Jim McCarthy from the Alert Engine Company, and I went along. We were all lightweights. When we went into the apartment, we came upon an unconscious woman who had overdosed. She had a history of depression, and she weighed at least four hundred pounds. Luckily, we had Joe Oswald as a cop at the scene. He was a heavy weight that could do heavy lifting.

Ed somehow knew that this woman was spiraling down the tubes and said that we had to get her out of the apartment and into the bus without delay. Joe carried her out by the feet, and Ed and I carried her at the head. Ed and I were both so thin, we had little trouble fitting together through the doorways. As we put her on the trundle, she went into cardiac arrest. Ed acted as if he'd known this was going to happen. As usual, he kept his cool and just started doing what had to be done. When we got her into the ambulance, I worked the ventilations. I inserted an esophageal tube airway to block the stomach contents from getting into the lungs. I then inserted the Levine tube down the airway, so that when the stomach contents evacuated, they would go through the Levine tube and not into her mouth and lungs. Jim was on compressions, and Ed was communicating to Medical Control after setting up an IV line. The vomit escaped through the Levine tube and onto the floor. The vomit was swishing on the floor with every sharp turn the ambulance made, but we were only paying attention to what we were doing and did not see the mess it was making until several minutes later.

We got her to the hospital, where she was pronounced dead. When we got home, we took the ambulance out of service for the better part of an hour. We put the vehicle nose-up on the driveway apron leading to the firehouse, opened the rear doors, and then hosed the inside, disinfecting the patient compartment before finally putting the bus back in service.

Baby Turning Blue

OVER THE MANY YEARS THAT I spent in the department, I responded to several calls for a babies who had stopped breathing. I would race to the call and find that the child was breathing but having a convulsion. Other calls that sounded upsetting were those that came over for children choking; you always had to expect an airway obstruction. In many of those calls, it turned out that before the first responder arrived at the scene, the airway obstruction was dislodged.

I remember one call that came over for a child choking. It was not far from where Garry Gronert lived, so he raced to the scene from his house. Upon his arrival, he came upon a five-year-old boy sitting in a chair and breathing normally. The child was, in fact, choking, but the obstructing mechanism had been dislodged prior to Garry's arrival. The boy did not have a tear in his eye.

When he met Garry, he put his hand out to shake hands and said, "My name is Kevin. I go to kindergarten."

Garry got a kick out of the kid. After the parents signed a refusal form for transportation to the hospital and further medical treatment, Garry came out of the house and told the story to the guys.

He was glad that it was nothing serious, adding, "The kid told me he goes to kindergarten. That is funny."

Another time, a call came over for a baby turning blue. As mentioned, we had gotten a lot of calls for children who had stopped breathing, but it often turned out that the child would start breathing again before our arrival. But this call came with a unique message: it was for a child *turning blue*. I knew this was not good.

I responded in the ambulance. On the way, a chief came through on the radio to tell us that we were responding to an infant in cardiac arrest. Ed Rothenberg lived nearby, so he was one of the first firemen on the scene. I walked into the house and the baby was lying on the dining room floor. Ed was doing CPR. It was a four-month-old infant. When we put the baby in the ambulance, Ed had me doing compressions. It looked and felt like a doll in my arms. Meanwhile, Ed ventilated the child with the infant bag valve mask. Upon arriving at Long Island Jewish Hospital, we passed the baby to Venard Brooks after he opened the rear doors of the bus. Venard walked into the ER while doing routine infant CPR. He put his mouth over the baby's nose and mouth, blowing in light puffs of air, and using his index and middle fingers to do compressions.

After we transferred the tiny patient to the hospital staff, I went outside to clean up the ambulance. Venard was outside by the ambulance. He lit a cigarette. At this point, his eyes welled up with tears. He walked to the other side of the ambulance so nobody could see him cry.

The next day, I saw Donald Phillips, who was in Rescue and who was also a dispatcher for the police department. I asked him for an update and he told me that they had gotten the baby to breathe again, but they did not expect the infant to live. The baby succumbed a few days later.

Later, my mother caught me brooding about this call, and said, "Don't be dwelling over this. The child is now an angel in heaven."

Super Blow Sunday

ANOTHER ROUTINE CALL WAS FOR a gas leak. That was when someone reported the smell of natural gas and we got called out. We responded to the scene. We called the gas company to turn the gas off. We went back home. This was the routine we followed for a gas leak over and over again.

However, one day, on a Super Bowl Sunday, when everyone was looking forward to watching the game, a call came over for a gas leak at the bowling alley on Tulip Avenue. It was a general alarm, so all companies responded to the scene. The chief in charge of the operation was Bill Green from the Active Engine Company. He called for an evacuation of the apartments above the bowling alley. After the apartments were evacuated, he called for all firemen to leave the building at once.

Then the inevitable happened. The whole building exploded. Two of our firemen were hurt. Thank God, none seriously. One was a fireman from the Reliance Engine Company, and the other was from the Hook and Ladder Company. The fireman from Reliance was Firefighter Matassa who had a nozzle hit him in the face. The other was Firefighter Paul Pinto from the Hook and Ladder Company. He was thrown by the explosion, and a flying brick hit him in the leg causing his leg to fracture. They were both hospitalized.

Marylou Norman from Rescue said that she prayed no firemen were left in the building when she saw the explosion. She was relieved to learn that the building had been completely evacuated.

After the explosion, Chief Green ordered the evacuation of all private homes in close proximity to the fire scene, as there was still some gas leakage coming from the street. They used a nearby high school to house the residents who had to flee. I could not read Chief Green's mind, but I guessed that he was thinking about the gas leak in Jamaica Queens, in which several blocks of private homes had exploded into flames. Not a soul had been hurt in that situation, because the homes had been evacuated in time. So it was a good call by Chief Green to evacuate the neighborhood, just to be safe.

It took the whole day and the whole night to put the fire out. There were half a dozen fire departments from neighboring towns and villages that were called in for mutual aid. All we could do at that point was to surround and drown the fire. The gas leak came from gas main on Tulip Avenue that we just let burn, because if that fire were extinguished, there would have been an accumulation of gas and we would have risked another explosion. Late that night, the Long Island Lighting Company shut the gas off and it stopped the leak in the street. There was not much more that we could do at that point, so we were finally put on a Signal 13.

The following April, when it was time for Chief Green to retire as chief of the department, he made a heart-wringing speech at the instillation dinner, thanking everyone for supporting him. He expressed appreciation for our sacrifices, and then he called up some of the firemen to receive awards; firefighters Pinto and Matassa were among them. They were the two who had been injured by the explosion.

When Pinto approached the front with a cast on his leg and using crutches, Chief Green said, "This is what I mean by sacrifices." He continued his speech, even getting choked up himself at times.

His company, the Active Engine Company, had a separate firehouse away from headquarters, but headquarters was where his chief's office was located. Therefore, he ended his speech by telling all of the members from the Active Engine Company, "When there is a call, leave a space for me on the back step of the truck, because I will be coming back home."

JOB CHANGE

ONE DAY IN THE MAIL, I received a letter saying I'd been called for the New York State Court Officer position. I had taken the written test in 1982, and in 1983 they had started hiring. At that time, Garry Gronert, who was a court officer, told me that he expected me to be called. It wasn't going to be in the first class in the academy but maybe in the following year or two. However, the hiring had been stopped for a year because of discrimination suits.

Then, sometime in the mid-1980s, they started hiring again. Garry was more optimistic than I that I would be hired. When I got called in the spring of 1986, I took the medical, physical agility, and psychological tests, and was assigned an investigator. I did not make it high enough on the list to get hired that year.

In the early spring of 1987, I went for another medical test, since it had been a year since my first one. I was interviewed for the psychological exam by a psychologist. Then, I waited to hear. It was late spring of that year when I received a letter saying that I had passed all of my screening tests and that I would be considered for appointment when they reached my list number, which would be soon. I felt more optimistic this time. I told Garry the good news. But then he became more pessimistic. He asked me if I had been called for the July class, and I told him that I hadn't been, but that I'd been told I would be considered in the near future.

"Hmm," he said, "well at least you have a job."

He thought that the list would be exhausted after the July class, but later told me that there was going to be another class in September. At this point, I was getting anxious. I received canvass letters with offers from Nassau County, but turned them down, since they were only for temporary positions. Then one day, I returned to the post office after completing my route and was told that I had a phone call. I answered and it was someone from the courts asking if I was interested in a permanent position as a court officer in the New York City Courts. I said yes without hesitation.

The man on the line gave me instructions on what to wear and bring with me, and then the last thing he said to me was, "Congratulations, and welcome aboard."

My first day at the academy was September 8, 1987. Today, a new court officer must spend four months in the academy. Back when I first started, it was only the better part of three weeks. Then we went for training in firearms and first aid after being on the job for six months.

My first assignment was in the Queens Criminal Court. I graduated from the academy on September 25, 1987, and had my first day in court on September 28. During that time period, I started to get muscle pain in my left groin. I believed it was probably from the physical training that I had done in the academy. Day by day, however, it got worse, and I was on probation, so I could not call in sick.

Finally, on October 9, which was a Friday, my neighbor drove me to Long Island Jewish Hospital because I thought that I had a femoral hernia. After being examined by the doctor, I received a prescription for an anti-inflammatory called Indomethacin. He told me that if I felt relief by the next day, then I had been right the first time—it was only a pulled muscle. If I didn't get relief, he said, I should seek medical help because it could be a hernia. I went home, took the medication, and went to bed. The next morning, I woke up with my groin feeling as good as new. Therefore, it was just a strain. I felt relieved to know that it was not a hernia and that I didn't need to take any time off from my new job.

As far as the fire department was concerned, I was out of commission during this minor crisis. I showed Captain Mahler the discharge papers from the hospital to be excused for the time I was out. My average was a little low, however, so I would soon have to try to boost it a little. In or around November of 1988, I received a warning letter in the mail stating that my average was delinquent. This was the first of the three strikes. I was seriously thinking of transferring to the Active Engine Company, which didn't have as many calls and was right across the street from my house. Either that or maybe resign completely.

In late November or early December, I went on a routine rescue call and took the ride to the hospital. I don't even remember the nature of the call; I was just trying to pull up my average. When I went, I told Ed Rothenberg about my letter.

"Don't worry about it," he said. "They are reducing the minimum average for Rescue down to fifteen percent, as opposed to twenty-five percent, anyway."

Mike Gerbaisi, who was the captain said, "We squelched the letters because some people were above that fifteen percent for the quarter ending in September, but below twenty-five percent,"

I told Ed that I was contemplating either transferring or resigning. He talked me into staying in Rescue. "Come to the meeting next Wednesday," he said, "and you will hear about the changes."

At the meeting, Mike Gerbaisi was the captain, Venard Brooks was the first lieutenant, and Jim Hickman was the second lieutenant.

Someone walked in late, and Mike said, "You are late, and your shoes are untied."

There was an outburst of laughter. Mike was a bit of a clown the way he ran meetings. After a few years of low morale and animosity among many, however, the company needed a clown like him. That way people would think, "Gee, this guy is funny. I'm going to make more meetings. I'm going to make more drills. I'm going to make more calls." Morale started to skyrocket in an upward fashion.

As for our chief, Mike Ostipwko, he hadn't been treated right when he'd first become a chief. This was the time he got his well-deserved break.

When the meeting was over, Jim Hickman pointed out a table that had been set up in the room. "We have a card table for anyone who wants to play poker and see if we can add to the camaraderie in the company."

I then saw something that I had not seen in a long time. People were laughing and joking instead of acting out the chips on their shoulders.

In addition to Mike Gerbaisi being like a comedian, Jim Hickman, Venard Brooks, and another asset to the company, Scott Baker, all made a fun team and brought the company together. They took advantage of every little bit of fun we could have together. Another asset to the company at that time was Carolyn Wood. She was like a loving kid sister to a lot of us. Many tried to imitate her general compassion for our brother and sister members. Members from other companies who once hated us were now complimenting us for this tremendous improvement in our group.

We thought the next chief, Phil Friedman, would screw us in every way he could, but we were wrong. At fire calls, he gave our company tasks to help out, and he spoke highly of us in a lot of ways. He respected us and acted like we were just great.

About a week later, we decided to go Christmas caroling. Jim Hickman played Santa, and we went around on the rescue truck playing Christmas songs and giving candy canes out to little kids. I had been a court officer for a little more than a year by that time, and the next month marked my tenth anniversary of being in Rescue.

Back in Action

At the turn of the new year of 1988, my AMT certification ran out. I tried to get into a refresher course that would cover both EMT and AMT certifications, but it used to be that you would have to take two separate courses to maintain both certifications. So I was mistakenly put in an EMT refresher course that had no AMT training in it. I learned that it was not going to be until spring that I would see a course that had both, however, so I just became EMT-certified. By the end of 1988, after a big morale boost, people were starting to like themselves again.

In early 1989, even though I had the minimum qualification as an EMT and still had two years left on my EMT certification, I decided I would enroll in a combined EMT/AMT refresher course. On the first day of the course, I ran into Rickie Maickels. He had not been very active in the company for a few years, but for some reason, he had decided to come back. Since Rickie was an ex-chief, he did not have to keep an average. Therefore, they could not penalize Rickie for not being around the past few years. Now, we were going to classes together and talking about the old days when I first came in the company. He had been in the company since May of 1971 and I since January of 1979. We both admitted to being a little rusty with our skills.

When the course was over, I noticed Rickie showing up at calls more often. One early evening, when the weather was starting to get a little warmer, we responded to a call for a man having a heart attack while on the roof of a private residence. Both the truck and the ambulance responded to the scene. We took a ladder off of the truck along with the boat, a basket-like stretcher normally called a stokes basket; somehow, we had come to nickname it "the boat." At the house, a few of us climbed the ladder to the roof with the boat. Rickie and I were among them. The man was conscious, but in distress. We put him on oxygen and placed him in the boat. I tied two clove hitches from two separate ropes, and then I handed the ropes to at least two of our guys inside the house through a window.

This was done to prevent the boat from falling off of the roof with the patient inside. If the boat decided to go, the men inside the house would hold the ropes and keep the boat from falling.

We got the patient inside the house through a window, and then we untied the ropes and put them aside. After that, the easy part came. Rickie and another member carried the patient, who was still secured in the boat, down the stairs to put him in the ambulance. I looked at Rickie doing what he was doing, and thought "That's how you regain confidence after being off the saddle for some time." As I mentioned before, we both had diminished confidence from not being around as much anymore. We both had admitted to being kind of rusty with our skills. Somehow, though, when you got back into the action like this, you learned that picking up your skills from the past was just like riding a bicycle: it just came back to you.

Another case that I had, which I hadn't had in a long time, was a motor vehicle accident. The patient on the scene was standing up, talking to the cop and complaining of neck pain. There were just two of us in the ambulance—Carolyn Woods was driving and I was riding shotgun, and that was it. Carolyn was fairly new, but she was trained. If I remember correctly, she had taken an EMT course in the same building and at the same time as Rickie Maickels and I had taken the refresher course. She also kept a low profile and was warm- hearted and compassionate, so I knew I could get along with her in this stressful moment.

As we approached the scene, I assumed that this patient would be very cooperative and easy to take care of. I was reminded about a case we'd had in which a man had fallen off the roof of his house, but refused to be immobilized with a spine board. He just walked to the trundle, lay down on it, and said he was all right. We found out from the hospital later that the guy had had a fractured spine and was lucky he wasn't paralyzed. So in that moment when Carolyn and I were approaching the scene, I was thinking we would just put a cervical collar on the patient, with no spinal immobilization, as that was the standard procedure in such a case. Instead, they wanted us to give him the whole works. We had to put on a cervical collar and use a spine board to immobilize his spine. Carolyn and I did a rapid take-down. I put traction on the patient's neck and Carolyn put a cervical collar on him. Then she put the spine board behind the patient while he was still standing up. We had the patient lean back on the spine board and then we gently lowered him to the ground in a lying position. Finally, we put him on the trundle and into the ambulance. The recent training that Carolyn and I had paid off. As I said, it just comes back to you no matter how long you've been away.

Man in the Bathtub

One evening while I was driving home from work, a call came over my pager for an unconscious man over at the Tulip Avenue apartments. I was just around the corner from the firehouse, so I drove there and rode in the ambulance to the scene. I had the pleasure of working with another probationary member, Michael Vessichio. He was a good kid. He was trying to show initiative and get experience just like all of us had done at one time. This time I wasn't alone with the new person, though. I had other experienced members on board. But like I said, Mike was a good kid. He was dependable, but still a little green.

As we were walking into the apartment complex where the call was, I saw one of our guys from across the street running to the scene. This guy was the type who thought that when the pager went off, he was the only one who could save the patient. He was a real egotist. So when I saw him, I thought, "Well, well. Now the world is saved."

When Mike and I entered the apartment, we were directed to the bathroom. The egotist beat me there, pulling me away from the bathroom door and entering. He, of course, was the best man for the job. When he saw what was inside, however, he covered his mouth with his hand and pulled me back in. There was an unconscious man in the bathtub who had defecated all over himself. The water in the tub was brown with feces. The situation was kind of strange. The man was naked from the waist down, but had a blue sweater on. Mike and I literally had to go into the bathtub and get our clothes wet with the feces-infested water, to get the patient out of the tub. Mike took the head and I took the feet. When we picked him up, we were splashed with even more water. We put him on the Reeves stretcher, onto the trundle, and into the ambulance.

I remember Kevin Kelleher and Ray Neufeld were on the call also. In the ambulance, Kevin set up the MAST suit, since the patient's blood pressure was low. Mike and I wrapped the suit onto the patient and then Mike pumped the suit to inflate it. This was supposed to elevate the patient's blood pressure, in treatment for shock.

Mike stopped inflating the suit and said, "Okay, it is at three fifty."

Kevin shouted, "That's classroom shit! Pump until you hear the Velcro snap!"

We finally arrived at Winthrop Hospital. Mike and I stunk like mules. Ray Neufeld was writing out the paperwork for the hospital.

"Ew, I smell," I said.

Ray said, "I agree with you. You really do stink. Could you stand someplace else?"

Mike and I both made the ambulance stink the whole way home from the hospital and probably for a while after. When I got home from that call, I quickly took off my contaminated clothes and went right into the shower.

A few days later we had a social gathering at the firehouse, and Kevin Kelleher told me that the man from the bathtub had died. We were having a few beers, so I was not sorting out my words correctly in response to his news.

"How bad was he?" I asked Kevin, wanting to know what he had died from

Kevin replied, "He's dead."

"I know, but how bad was he?" I repeated.

Kevin exclaimed, "He's dead!"

Chief Frank Wakely was laughing. "He's only a little dead, but thank God he's not too badly dead."

That was the typical firehouse humor that went on. Finally, I rephrased my question, asking what was wrong with him to cause him to die, but Kevin did not have any more information.

Another memorable winter call, which happened in early 1989, was for a downed man at the A&P Supermarket on Jericho Turnpike. I responded with a crew in the ambulance. Sure enough, the patient was in cardiac arrest. I remember doing ventilations. Meanwhile, Ray Neufeld came in with the defibrillator. It used to be that you could not defibrillate unless it was ordered by Medical Control, but by this time, they had changed the protocol, allowing us to defibrillate on standing orders—or, in other words, without their approval. This showed how the protocols changed from time to time, and for a lot of us, it was hard to keep up with, which is why we had to refresh our certification every three years.

At any rate, Ray put the paddles on the person and found that he was in ventricular fibrillation. He then ordered us to resume CPR for another minute. After the minute, I heard him say, "Clear." He then put the paddles on the patient's chest and shocked him. In just one shock, he brought the patient back to a normal Sinus Rhythm. We put the patient in the ambulance, and, with Ray on board, I continued to ventilate on the way to the hospital. Finally, the patient started to breathe on his own. He was still unconscious, however, when we left him at the hospital.

There was no further news on the patient's condition, but then we only got bad news if the patient died, so we figured, in this case, no news was good news. After losing the patient from the bathtub call, it was a good feeling to see someone brought back like that. That was the first time I saw a cardiac arrest patient get shocked on standing orders.

It's Always a Pleasure

"It's always a pleasure to work a call with my buddy Danny." That is what Jim Norman used to say about me. Jim came into the company in 1985 along with his sister Marylou. The thing I remember most about Jim is that I did a lot of partying with him. One night that sticks in my mind is when we were at Archie Cheng's Captain's Dinner together, at Koenig's Restaurant. That night, Jim and I closed down a few local taverns after Archie's affair.

Jim never had a bad thing to say about anyone. "Isn't he a good kid?" he'd say. Or, "Isn't she nice?" Or, "That person is valuable to the company." These were the things that Jim said about people—everything was positive. One night, I was at a bar talking with him and he told me, "Dan, you're not good and you're not bad. You're excellent." Come to think of it, he was one of the people who had talked me into staying in Rescue when I was contemplating leaving.

Another memorable occasion was the 1989 New Year's Eve party run by the Hook and Ladder Company. All I remember was that a lot of us were completely smashed and that Jim's wife drove me home that night—or, maybe I should say early the next morning.

The day after that party, we had about six rescue calls. I was off from work that day, so I made just about all of them. One came over back-to-back with another, so some of us were ordered to go to the hospital with the patient on the first call, while others had to take the patient in the second. I rode to the second call with Reliance Engine Company Chief Phill Friedman.

As we raced to the location, I remember Phill saying, "Boy, Danny, your average is skyrocketing through the roof."

When the quarter was over at the end of March of that year, my average had climbed to 35 percent, all the way from 19 percent at the end of December. As mentioned, the new requirement was 15 percent, which they had imposed not too long before that time.

The next New Year's Eve party, for the year 1990, we had a blast just as we had the year before, although the 1989 party was more memorable. Before the 1991 New Year's Eve party, all Jim and I were talking about was how drunk we were going to get that night, but we not only ended up not drinking that night, but also missing the countdown because we had several back-to-back rescue calls to attend to.

When we got back to the firehouse after the round of calls, we went upstairs to the ballroom, and everyone was going home. Some people were staggering out the door. I could not believe my eyes. Everything was clear, and I wasn't seeing double like I had at the previous New Year's Eve parties.

For the next week or so, while talking about the party and the calls we had to go to, all I heard Jim telling people was, "Danny was as sober as a judge."

Another memorable call I had with Jim was back in 1989. I was on my way home when I heard a call for a house fire come over my pager. I responded in my car and, upon my arrival, I met Chief Wakley, who had also just arrived at the scene. There wasn't a lot of visible fire from where we were standing, but there was the strong smell of smoke. We went into the house. It looked like a normal house. The lights were on and there was no fire or smoke. The homeowner then led us up the stairs. At the top of the staircase was a drop ladder coming down from the ceiling. We learned that the fire was in the attic. Chief Wakley wouldn't dare open up the attic door, for fear of a back draft.

"Dan," Chief Wakley said, "go outside, meet your truck, and gear up, because we have work to do."

I ran outside and the rescue truck was just arriving. Chief of Department Phill Friedman was in charge of the operation. The Ladder Company had to vent the house while the Pumper Company stood by with a hose line at the top of the stairs where the drop ladder was. Once the Ladder Company had opened up a hole in the roof above the attic, it was safe for the Pumper Company to open the drop ladder and attack the fire. It was one of those jobs where they could not get the fire out quickly, but had it well under control.

Meanwhile, Chief Friedman ordered Jim Norman and I to climb a ladder that ran up the outside of the house, to a window that led to the attic. We were then to break the glass to add to the ventilation. Jim and I went up but didn't go inside the window, because we would have to assist with overhaul after the fire was under control. We did a leg lock on the rung we were on to prevent us from falling. As soon as we broke the window, we were getting wet, as the water being sprayed inside was splashing on us. Finally, the fire seemed to go out, but there was a rekindle, which happened because there were many years of junk accumulation in the attic. Once the rekindle was put out, the men in the house handed Jim and I one piece of junk at a time to throw down to the ground. At first I felt my fear of heights come back, but after awhile I got used to it.

When we were waiting for the next piece of debris to come out, Jim said, "It's always a pleasure to work on a call with my buddy Danny."

Finally, we were put on a Signal 13.

As mentioned before, everyone in Rescue had thought that Chief Phill Friedman would be against Rescue and that he would do everything he could to screw us. We were wrong. After our morale boost, Phill became impressed and was good enough to give fire jobs to members of Rescue, as he had to both Jim and I that night.

That is what Jim and I were saying while we were up on those ladders, assisting in the removal of debris. Rescue did not always get the chance to participate in fires because our main job was to tend to medical emergencies. Not too many other chiefs would have given us that opportunity.

Shot in the Foot

One night I was in bed trying to get to sleep. Before I dozed off, a call came over as a gunshot wound. I recognized the address as one of the cops in town. Fortunately, he had moved from that house prior to this incident; however, I didn't know that at the time, and responded to the call hoping that the patient wouldn't be him.

When I arrived at the scene, I saw the patient sitting on the stoop. It wasn't the cop I knew, thank God. This patient seemed calm, cool, and collected. He complained that he had been shot in the foot as the result of a robbery attempt. As I delicately removed his shoe, he was telling us that he had been stopped at a stop sign near the Bellerose Train Station when someone had pulled a gun on him. He'd struggled to get the gun away from the robber, and a shot rang out, wounding him in the foot. For some reason, that didn't sound right at all. For starters, he was not a bit upset.

After I removed his shoe, I saw a wound on top of his foot, below the toes. It went all the way through the bottom of his foot. That is, the entrance wound was on the top of his foot and the exit wound was on the sole. There was not much blood. I just dressed the wound, and when the ambulance arrived, we immobilized his foot with a splint over the dressing.

I had only seen a few gunshot wounds that had resulted in a lot of blood. One was at the call at the hotel, when the man had been shot in his femoral artery. Another time, I had an off-duty cop accidently shoot himself in the index finger. He was trying to holster the weapon with his finger around the trigger, and the holster had pushed his trigger-finger back, making him accidently squeeze the trigger. He didn't lose the finger. There was just a smooth entrance and exit wound. Another time I had a man accidently shoot himself in the leg. It was at the Tulip Avenue Firing Range. He had an entrance wound on the inner side of his thigh and an exit wound on the outer side of his shin. Even in that case, there was not much blood.

Getting back to the man who said he'd been robbed, they took him to the hospital. I was to stay back, and after I was released, I went back home and went back to bed. As I lay down to sleep, I heard the sound of a police helicopter. It was apparent they were looking for the robber.

A few days later, I was not surprised to hear what had really happened. His girlfriend had been an off-duty cop and was present at the scene. It turned out that he was playing with her police revolver and accidently shot himself in the foot. The robbery story was a hoax. After he went to the hospital, the police had to investigate further and the girlfriend was asked a lot of questions. Eventually, they found out the truth, but the girlfriend faced repercussions from the police department. The lesson to be learned: nothing is worth lying about.

The End of the Road

THE YEAR 1992 STARTED OFF just like any other year. It started with the New Year's Eve party, and from there, life was just the normal routine. In the middle of February, Carolyn Woods became Mrs. James Hickman. I went to their wedding. At the end of February, I went to my union dentist to have a tooth problem taken care of. When I came home, my mother told me that the father of one of my childhood friends was murdered. He was shot in the face with a shotgun while driving to work.

Since I was friends with the son of the deceased, the police questioned me. They questioned me in a harsh way, as if I were trying to hide something. They did the same to a lot of people who were close to my friend. I was even told by my union that I could lose my job if I did not cooperate, which never happened, but the threat itself brought on a lot of stress. I would say that it even turned into paranoia. I didn't treat it because I thought that the anxiety would go away in time.

That all started at the end of February, and by the beginning of June that year, my mind started to have what is known as racing thoughts. There were one million thoughts going through my mind all at once. I lost my ability to concentrate on my normal daily routine. I was having a nervous breakdown.

They noticed the deterioration in my personality at work. Therefore, I was hospitalized. I spent four weeks in the hospital and was discharged at the beginning of July.

The police also had to investigate people from the deceased person's job. To this day, there have been no arrests made related to his murder, and it remains a cold case. But the whole thing made me depressed. For the better part of two years, I felt constant depression.

In December of 1992, I was sent home from work for a couple of days. I was functional but depressed, and my concentration was not as good as it had been prior to the ordeal. My psychiatrist said that I was over medicated and adjusted the dosage. While I was home, the guys and gals from Rescue stopped at my house with the truck. They were Christmas caroling. I answered the door and invited them in.

Ed Rothenberg pulled me out the door by the arm, and said, "No, you're coming out."

I went in the truck and rode around with them. It was the usual Christmas caroling tradition. We played Christmas songs on the PA system and handed out candy canes to children.

Of course, Jim Norman put his arm around me and asked, "How's my buddy Danny doing?"

"Okay," I said. I really was not myself. I felt down. All I did was look out the window and stare into space.

Marty Cook sat down to talk to me. "Sometimes these people in the psychology profession can serve to make you feel worse."

I definitely agreed with him at the time. My mental well- being was beginning to look like a jigsaw puzzle that I had to put back together again.

After being discharged from the hospital, I had taken a leave of absence from the fire department. I had to avoid stress. But now I was starting to get back into action. I went to a call here and a call there, and was slowly getting back into the swing of things.

In the spring of 1993, we celebrated the one hundredth anniversary of the Floral Park Fire Department. I still felt depressed. By this time, I thought my depression was never going to go away. It had been a year since I'd had my breakdown, and I felt that I wasn't getting any better.

In May of 1994, after having my medication reduced over a year's time, the dosage had been whittled down to practically nothing. I started to have racing thoughts again. As a result, I was hospitalized a second time. When I first arrived at the hospital, they gave me a shot to help me sleep. It was around 10:00 in the morning. I slept around the clock and awoke around 7:00 in the morning. I woke up to the sight of a nice, compassionate nurse telling me I could get up and walk around the unit. I felt like a different person. My depression was gone. The bad thing about that good feeling was that I thought I had been cured and needed no further treatment. Fortunately, that thought was followed up by the more rational thought that I needed to stay on my medication.

After two weeks in the hospital, I was discharged. The first time I had been released from the hospital, I had been able to go to work right away. This time I had to arrange to be examined by a state doctor before returning to work. There was a lot of red tape, but I got through it. I was off for the whole summer. I needed the time off to get my head back together. I still had to avoid stress, but again started to increase the number of calls I went on. I took advantage of the time off from work to do just that.

One evening, during this leave from work, I was driving down Jericho Turnpike. A call came over for an unconscious woman. I was close by, so I responded directly to the scene. I arrived at the same time as Floral Park Police Officer Dennis Nicholson. We ran up the stairs to the bedroom where the patient was. Well, so much for avoiding stress. We came upon an elderly woman in full cardiac arrest. What was I getting myself into? Dennis gave me a mask to get started on ventilations. I was able to handle myself all right. For the first time in my life, I did one-man CPR on the woman until the bus arrived. All of the other times that I'd done CPR, I'd had a partner. We put the woman in the ambulance and hooked her up to the monitor. We got a Brady Rhythm—a slow pulse under sixty beats per minute. The woman's pulse rate had previously been down to thirty beats per minute. Kevin Kelleher, with the assistance of Stephanie Cook, put an external pacemaker on the woman. This brought her pulse rate up enough to sustain her life. The woman was admitted to the hospital as a save on our part.

Avoid stress? No way. This was a good feeling and was even kind of therapeutic for me. The stress that had put me in the hospital was paranoia caused by a criminal investigation and the way it had affected my job as a court officer; but that paranoia had not precluded me from administering first aid or fighting fires.

That year, Jim Norman told me that everyone saw a different person in me. He said that I had developed twice the confidence that I'd had before that second hospitalization. I just continued therapy and maintained my medication and was able to return to work the day after Labor Day.

I was pretty much back into the swing of things at work and at the Rescue Company. I did the usual routine. I went to work and answered as many calls as I could until my mother had to go in for heart surgery, at which point I had to take some time off from the fire department. My mother came home from the hospital after a three-month ordeal, at which point I was able to answer some calls again. That was at the end of 1995.

The following year, 1996, was pretty normal until I came home from work one day and my mother said, "You have to get a lawyer, because this is getting to be harassment."

I didn't know what she was talking about until she showed me the letter. I and about thirty other people had received a letter from the police asking yet more questions about the still-unsolved homicide that they thought my friend had been involved with.

I didn't think anything was wrong, but everyone told me to hire a lawyer. That was in early December. By the end of the month, I hired a lawyer. I had been doing fine until I'd had to ask my superiors at work to give me a letter stating that I was at work on the day in question. Then it started to get nerve-racking. When I asked for the letter on Friday, January 3, 1997, I was ordered to appear in the office on the morning of Monday, January 6, 1997. I was perplexed, but thought I could handle myself all right. That Saturday, I made a mistake. I didn't take my medication. On Sunday, I felt those racing thoughts again. This wasn't good. Sure enough, on Monday, I was hospitalized for the third time. This was to be the final time I was hospitalized.

The first time I was examined to go back to work, I was found unfit. Therefore, I was out of work for sixteen months. I realized during that time that the common denominator of all of my hospitalizations was that they had all happened as the result of stress from work. I had had other occasions on which I had talked to the police, with no repercussions in my mental status. I wasn't so much afraid of the police. I knew that I had told them all I knew, which was nothing good enough to cause them to make an arrest. It was my job that I was afraid for.

During my leave from work, I was pretty active in the Rescue Company. Finally I was able to return to work after being reexamined. Since these hospitalizations had happened while I was at work, however, the big boss in Manhattan took me out of the Queens Criminal Court and put me in Brooklyn Criminal Court.

On my first day back, he said, "Putting you in Brooklyn is not punishment in any way. It is just to get you away from whatever it was that was bothering you in Queens."

I was afraid of Brooklyn at first. However, I adjusted almost immediately. I liked the staff and nearly the whole staff liked me.

On the other hand, my fire department average went down. As a result, in November of 1998, I had to answer to the Fire Council, which was made up of all five chiefs in the department. Bob Hayes was my captain, and he was suggesting that I go into an associate membership, which you qualify for when you have either twenty years of service or ten years of service with a medical condition. I was in the homestretch of having twenty years; the following January would be my twentieth anniversary. The council went into executive session, and I had to leave the room.

Bob Hayes came out to get me when the session was over. He put both thumbs up and whispered, "This is good."

When I reentered the room, Chief Mike Green told me that I could stay active and that they were giving me a six-month probation period to help me bring up my average and help me get back into the swing of things.

From that point on, I tried to stay active for as long as possible. And I agreed with myself that I would not stay active if I couldn't do a good job. Then on January 8, 1999, I had my anniversary, which qualified me to become an associate member.

Spring of 1999 came and we had a call that came over for someone with difficulty breathing. I responded in my car since I was driving home and was not close enough to the firehouse to make the ambulance. When I arrived at the scene, the patient was already being carried down a flight of stairs. I looked at the patient and it was not good. I heard the crackling sounds of fluids in the lungs, which meant that he was in pulmonary edema.

While they were transferring him to the trundle, I went into the ambulance and set up the ambu-bag. I knew that we were going to have to resuscitate. He was positioned with his shoulders elevated, so he would not drown in his own fluids, but this made it difficult to do ventilations. He wasn't breathing, but he did have a pulse. CPR compressions were not necessary, but artificial respiration was desperately needed. I was standing in an awkward position, and the patient was not lying flat. Matt Dwyer was sitting on the opposite side of the trundle holding the mask sealed over the patient's nose and mouth. I squeezed the bag to force air into his lungs. Meanwhile, Ray Neufeld and Carol Ragona attempted to start an IV line. When we arrived at the hospital, the staff in the ER inserted an endotracheal tube.

This patient ended up walking out of the hospital. I had the pleasure of observing him in a grocery store on Tulip Avenue doing some shopping. I must say that all involved on the call did a good job—Ray and Carol in administering the IV line, and Matt and I on the ventilations. I had been in such an awkward position and standing up so I could reach the patient's head. Matt had held the mask over the nose and mouth to form a seal so I could get air into the patient's lungs. Ray had complimented me by saying, "That was a good call you did by setting up the ambu-bag." At that point in time, I did not know that this call would be my last spectacular save.

In July of 1999, during a tremendous heat wave, we had a call that came over for possible heat exhaustion. It was at a retirement residence at St. Hedwig's Church. We went into the apartment and found the man complaining of indigestion and gastric reflux. I knew that it wasn't heat exhaustion because he wasn't perspiring and the air conditioner in the apartment was working. We took him to Long Island Jewish Hospital. It was a good idea to transport him just to make sure it wasn't his heart. We stayed with him in the ER until he was signed in. Meanwhile, another patient on a hospital bed, who had a heat-related illness, leaned over the rail and vomited at my feet. Little did I know that this would be my last call as an active member of Rescue.

When we returned from the hospital, Carol Ragona, who was the company captain at the time, said, "Danny, you fell under average for the quarter ending in June. And guess what?"

I knew that I was going to have to appear before council. It was then that I decided to become an associate member. With associate membership, you do not have to answer calls any more. So I made this my last call ever. Then I waited for the August council meeting to arrive.

Epilogue

Before the council meeting, I asked Joe Reekie, who was an associate member, how to apply for associate membership. It was a simple procedure—a form of resignation from active duty and an application for associate membership all in one. I had to turn my pager in and take my turnout gear out of the truck. But I got to keep everything else, such as my uniform and keys to the firehouse.

The reason that my average had fallen so low was because, from February to May of that year, I had been studying for a promotion exam for the position of court clerk. I passed the test and eventually got the promotion in 2004. But it had been a tough test that had required a lot of studying, and I just hadn't had the time to answer fire and rescue calls. Besides that, I had been thinking that I had just about had it. Twenty years of seeing things like the man vomiting at my feet in the ER on my last call. Or the time we did extrication for a woman trapped in a car. The passenger door had been bent in and was crushing her leg. When we finally freed her and put her on the trundle, Kevin Kelleher cut off her boot and asked me to hand him an abdominal trauma pad. When I handed it to him, I noticed that he was holding her leg together. It looked as if almost her whole leg had been severed. There was arterial bleeding spurting out from several areas. He quickly put the dressing on to control the bleeding. Worse yet, her boyfriend had been killed in that accident. He was the driver and had been thrown into the backseat, hitting his head on the ceiling and breaking his C-spine.

As John Bennett, an associate member since the late 1980s, had said to me one day, during our long talk on the train on the way to work, "When you become a volunteer fireman, you have to really think about what you are doing. It doesn't put bread on the table, and it is dangerous. You can get hurt and there sometimes can be liability."

On the night of the council meeting, several members had the same problem as I did: their averages were low for the previous quarter.

The chiefs were willing to give all of us a fair shake. They realized that they, too, could fall under average.

When it was my turn, I walked in and all Chief Chuck Zuba said was, "Congratulations, you are accepted as an associate member." Then I was excused. I turned in all of my equipment.

Now I just live my busy life, working and taking care of my home. I felt kind of relieved from the responsibility of being a firefighter EMT. Before I worked full time, I had all the time in the world, but now, it would just be too much. I still see a lot of the other fire department guys, both active and retired. For years, John Bennett and Jim Norman tried to get me to go to Trinity Restaurant with some of the other former members of Rescue. I always said that I would, but never got around to it. Until one day.

John Bennett drove up to me while I was walking to the train station on my way to work and said, "We are going to Trinity tonight at 7:00. If you're not there, I am coming over to your house and I will drag you out."

So I went. And I continue to go. It's nice. I get to see a lot of my fellow old-timers. We tell war stories. We can tell gruesome stories, because we are in a private room in the back, away from people eating. I just wait for Marty's e-mail, and then I mark my calendar and just go.

Once you become a volunteer fireman, you can leave the fire department, but the fire department never leaves you.